IAN DAWSON

THE
WARS
of the
ROSES

**HODDER
EDUCATION**

AN HACHETTE UK COMPANY

Dedication

For Matt – in the hope that this is more understandable than Ma's thesis.

Acknowledgements

The author and publisher wish to thank John Watts for his unfailing help, courtesy and interest as Academic Consultant. All judgements, interpretations and errors remain the responsibility of the author.

Photo credits

Cover © Studio-Annika/iStockphoto; **p.2** *tl* © Museum of London, *tr* © Bibliothèque royale de Belgique; MS 9967, f.39r, *b* © Mike Booth/Alamy; **p.3** *t* © Nicholas Bailey/Rex Features, *c* © The Trustees of the British Museum, *b* © The British Library Board (Shelfmark Add. 43490 f.24); **p.5** *t* © Painting by Graham Turner www.studio88.co.uk, *b* © National Museum of Wales; **p.16** © English School/The Bridgeman Art Library/Getty Images; **p.19** © The British Library Board (Shelfmark Cotton Roll II (23)); **p.27** © 2008 INTERFOTO/Sammlung Rauch/Mary Evans; **p.51** © Rex Features; **p.52** © BL Images Ltd/Alamy; **p.53** © Chris Bland/Eye Ubiquitous/Corbis ; **p.54** © The British Library Board (Shelfmark Royal 15 E. VI, f.2v); **p.70** © Biological Anthropology Research Centre, Archaeological Sciences, University of Bradford; **p.76** © The Granger Collection, NYC/TopFoto; **p.80** © The Art Archive/Ashmolean Museum; **p.90** © The British Library Board (Shelfmark Royal 18 D. II, f.30v); **p.96** © The Trustees of the 9th Duke of Buccleuch's Chattels Fund; **p.99** © Topham/Woodmansterne/TopFoto; **p.104** © 2010 SuperStock; **p.107** Ms 265 f.VI v Edward IV, with Elizabeth Woodville, Edward V and Richard, Duke of Gloucester, later Richard III, from the 'Dictes of Philosophers', c.1477 (vellum) by English School, (15th century) © Lambeth Palace Library, London, UK/The Bridgeman Art Library; **p.112** © The British Library Board (Shelfmark Cotton Vespasian F. XIII f.123); **p.115** © The National Archives; **p.118** Ms.266 fol.10 Henry VII (1457–1509) king of England (1485–1509), from 'Recueil d'Arras' (pencil on paper) (b/w photo) by Le Boucq, Jacques (d.1573) © Bibliotheque Municipale, Arras, France/Giraudon/The Bridgeman Art Library; **p.121** Photo by Pat Dawson. Reproduced by the kind permission of the Earl and Countess of Harewood and Trustess of the Harewood House Trust; **p.124** © 2008 INTERFOTO/NG Collection/Mary Evans; **p.125** *l & r* © Bosworth Battlefield Heritage Centre; **p.132** © Pietro Torrigiano/The Bridgeman Art Library/Getty Images; **p.136** © Topham Picturepoint/TopFoto; **p.138** © Cadw, Welsh Assembly Government (Crown Copyright); **p.139** *l* © Painting by Graham Turner www.studio88.co.uk, *r* © The Art Archive/Private Collection/Philip Mould.

Text credits

p.17 Redrawn map, after A.J.Pollard, *Late Medieval England 1399-1509* (Longman, 2000); **p.32** Interview with Dr John Watts (Oxford University); **p.70** Table, after Colin Richmond, 'The Nobility and the Wars of the Roses 1459–1461', *Nottingham Medieval Studies, 21, 1977*, pp.71–85; **p.76** Christine Carpenter, from *The War of the Roses: Politics and the Constitution c.1437–1509* (Cambridge University Press, 1997), © Cambridge University Press 1997, reproduced by permission of the publisher.

Every effort has been made to trace all copyright holders, but if any have been inadvertently overlooked, the Publishers will be pleased to make the necessary arrangements at the first opportunity.

The Schools History Project

Set up in 1972 to bring new life to history for students aged 13–16, the Schools History Project continues to play an innovatory role in secondary history education. From the start, SHP aimed to show how good history has an important contribution to make to the education of a young person. It does this by creating courses and materials which both respect the importance of up-to-date, well-researched history and provide enjoyable learning experiences for students.

Since 1978 the Project has been based at Trinity and All Saints University College Leeds. It continues to support, inspire and challenge teachers through the annual conference, regional courses and website: http://www.schoolshistory project.org.uk. The Project is also closely involved with government bodies and awarding bodies in the planning of courses for Key Stage 3, GCSE and A level.

For teacher support material for this title, visit www.schools historyproject.org.uk.

Although every effort has been made to ensure that website addresses are correct at time of going to press, Hodder Education cannot be held responsible for the content of any website mentioned in this book. It is sometimes possible to find a relocated web page by typing in the address of the home page for a website in the URL window of your browser.

Hachette UK's policy is to use papers that are natural, renewable and recyclable products and made from wood grown in sustainable forests. The logging and manufacturing processes are expected to conform to the environmental regulations of the country of origin.

Orders: please contact Bookpoint Ltd, 130 Milton Park, Abingdon, Oxon OX14 4SB. Telephone: +44 (0)1235 827720. Fax: +44 (0)1235 400454. Lines are open 9.00a.m.–5.00p.m., Monday to Saturday, with a 24-hour message answering service. Visit our website at www.hoddereducation.co.uk.

© Ian Dawson 2012
First published in 2012 by
Hodder Education,
an Hachette UK company
338 Euston Road
London NW1 3BH

Impression number	10	9	8	7	6	5	4	3	2	1
Year		2016		2015		2014		2013		2012

Typeset in 10pt Usherwood Book
Layouts designed by Lorraine Inglis Design
Artwork by Oxford Designers and Illustrators and Barking Dog
Printed and bound in Italy

A catalogue record for this title is available from the British Library

ISBN 978 1 4441 4448 2

Contents

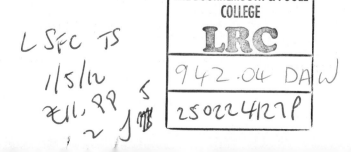

A window into the fifteenth century

We cannot visit the fifteenth century but we can catch glimpses of it through objects like these which were everyday sights for the people who lived in the time of the Wars of the Roses. These objects help us understand the ideals and interests of those people. The items are a reminder of their intelligence, literacy, wealth and beliefs. It would be quite wrong to think of them as 'thugs in armour'.

△ An everyday jug from the late 1400s

▽ Long Melford Church, Suffolk, much rebuilt in the 1400s

△ Fashionable courtiers in the 1460s

△ The effigy of Richard Beauchamp, Earl of Warwick who died in 1439: not just armour but a beautiful work of art

◁ A silver coin showing Edward IV

△ Letters were everyday objects, sent and received by the thousand in an increasingly literate society. This 'valentine' letter is from 1477

1 The Wars of the Roses: The essentials

Cannonballs hurtled through the air. Arrows arced into the sky, then screamed down into armour, flesh, bone. Foot-soldiers advanced, killing and maiming with sword or poll-axe, battle-lines blurring into a mass of fighting, desperate men. Suddenly, audible above the screeching clash of weapons, shouted orders, curses and screams, came the sound of hooves – hundreds of them, perhaps more – drumming on sun-hardened ground. Maybe the foot-soldiers paused, mid-combat, to watch the nerve-jangling, thrilling onrush of highly trained horses and armoured knights. At their head, now at full gallop, rode King Richard III, his banner displaying the royal Cross of St George and his personal badge, the white boar.

Crash! Richard and his knights careered into the bodyguard of their enemy, Henry Tudor. Richard's own lance killed William Brandon, Henry's standard-bearer. John Cheney, 'a giant of a man', blocked Richard's path but was hurled to the ground. Now Henry himself was desperately parrying Richard's blows. A few seconds more and Henry would be dead or a prisoner and then …

And then Richard and his knights realised they too were under attack as a third force charged in to defend Henry. Suddenly Henry was surrounded by protectors and out of reach of Richard's attack. Now it was Richard fighting for his life. Around him his knights were isolated and killed – his long-time friend, Robert Percy, his close advisers, Richard Ratcliffe and Robert Brackenbury, and other northern supporters. Then Richard himself was dragged or knocked from his horse. No surrender. No mercy. The thrust of a dagger or a crushing blow from a poll-axe ended the life of Richard III.

And far away from the battlefield, families waited, not knowing if they would ever see husbands, fathers or sons alive again. The battle of Bosworth did not simply add a new name to the list of English kings. It transformed the lives of wives, mothers, sons and daughters, friends and lovers – and ended the lives of those left lying in the bloody dust of the battlefield.

One of those waiting for news was Anne Herbert, Countess of Pembroke, portrayed on page 5 at home at Raglan Castle, Gwent. The news, when it came, was bad but could have been far worse. Anne's brother, Walter Devereux, had died fighting for Richard III but her sons, William and Walter, were alive.

If that sounds as if Anne experienced a rare mix of emotions in August 1485 there's more to come! Anne and her husband, William Herbert, had been guardians of the new king, Henry VII, when he'd been a boy and they'd planned for him to marry one of their daughters. Friendship with Henry may explain why Anne's sons did not fight for Richard at Bosworth, even though the elder, William, was married to Richard III's daughter.

These glimpses into one family's life show why the Wars of the Roses are so fascinating – it's the story of real people facing tough situations and difficult decisions. It's also an intriguing period because the fragmentary evidence creates many puzzles. To take just the example of Bosworth: was Richard III a murderous tyrant or a good, principled king or …? And why did men like Ratcliffe fight for Richard when others, like Cheney, risked life and lands by rebelling on behalf of Henry Tudor, a man even his own supporters hardly knew? There are many more such questions to come!

△ *Reverie* by Graham Turner, an imagined modern portrait of Anne Herbert, Countess of Pembroke.

Anne Herbert

Anne Herbert was born *c.*1433 and died sometime after 1485, so lived through the entire Wars of the Roses. Her husband, William, was executed after the battle of Edgecote in 1469, having fought for King Edward IV against the rebellious Earl of Warwick. The coat of arms on the window in the painting combines the Herbert lions and the coat of arms of Anne's family, the Devereux.

Why have we used an imagined portrait? It's not usual to include such a picture in this kind of book as we have no evidence of what Anne looked like. It's here as a reminder that the Wars of the Roses was a real event for people like Anne and to give you a sense of the period through her clothing, her book and the building itself.

Anne is shown in the Great Tower at Raglan Castle (see the picture of Raglan on page 53), probably in the 1460s when she was aged about 30. The artist, Graham Turner, bases his paintings on careful research, even taking up jousting to gain first-hand experience of weapons and armour to inform his paintings of battles and tournaments.

On pages 53 and 138–9 we will continue the story of the Herbert family during the 1400s.

◁ The Raglan Ring, found in 1968 near Raglan Castle. The design on the ring is of a lion – the Herbert badge – between the initials W and A, with an inscription 'Faithful to you'. To whom did it belong? The ring dates from *c.*1440–75 so it's tempting to say that it belonged to William Herbert, Earl of Pembroke whose wife, Anne, is shown above.

Have the Wars of the Roses got anything to do with Yorkshire and Lancashire?

No! Many people assume that the Wars of the Roses were fought between soldiers from the counties of Yorkshire and Lancashire. They weren't! Two families, the Yorkists and the Lancastrians, were at the heart of the fighting but they had lands all over the country. So forget about Yorkshire fighting Lancashire: that idea will only confuse you!

The Wars of the Roses: an outline, up to 1461

How long did the Wars of the Roses last and what was the overall pattern of events? Pages 6–9 help you understand the outline of the whole topic, perhaps the most important four pages in the book!

The pink boxes tell the story of events, while the graph shows how successful the kings were in achieving the objectives in the gold bars. If the line of the graph is high on the page then a king was successful; England was united and peaceful. If the graph falls to the bottom of the page then a king was a failure; war or rebellion had broken out.

Just reading these pages isn't enough to understand them. You need to transfer this information into your own version of the story. For example, can you tell this outline story aloud in your own words in 1 minute?

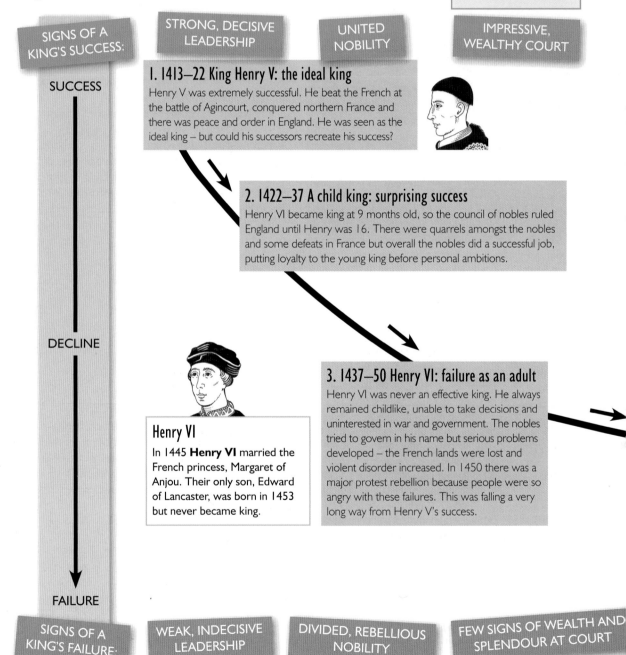

SIGNS OF A KING'S SUCCESS:

STRONG, DECISIVE LEADERSHIP

UNITED NOBILITY

IMPRESSIVE, WEALTHY COURT

SUCCESS

1. 1413–22 King Henry V: the ideal king
Henry V was extremely successful. He beat the French at the battle of Agincourt, conquered northern France and there was peace and order in England. He was seen as the ideal king – but could his successors recreate his success?

2. 1422–37 A child king: surprising success
Henry VI became king at 9 months old, so the council of nobles ruled England until Henry was 16. There were quarrels amongst the nobles and some defeats in France but overall the nobles did a successful job, putting loyalty to the young king before personal ambitions.

DECLINE

3. 1437–50 Henry VI: failure as an adult
Henry VI was never an effective king. He always remained childlike, unable to take decisions and uninterested in war and government. The nobles tried to govern in his name but serious problems developed – the French lands were lost and violent disorder increased. In 1450 there was a major protest rebellion because people were so angry with these failures. This was falling a very long way from Henry V's success.

Henry VI
In 1445 **Henry VI** married the French princess, Margaret of Anjou. Their only son, Edward of Lancaster, was born in 1453 but never became king.

FAILURE

SIGNS OF A KING'S FAILURE:

WEAK, INDECISIVE LEADERSHIP

DIVIDED, REBELLIOUS NOBILITY

FEW SIGNS OF WEALTH AND SPLENDOUR AT COURT

Essentials up to 1461

1. England was ruled successfully by the nobles while Henry VI was a child.
2. Henry VI completely failed to provide effective kingship when he grew up.
3. The first battle was about who would be Henry's chief councillor. It was NOT a battle for the crown.
4. In 1461 many nobles still wanted to keep Henry as king despite his failures but he was finally deposed by Edward of York.

STRONG DEFENCE AGAINST FRANCE AND SCOTLAND

LOW LEVELS OF CRIME AND DISORDER

SUCCESS

Henry VI was the third **Lancastrian** king. They are known as the House of Lancaster because Henry, his father (Henry V) and grandfather (Henry IV) were descended from the Dukes of Lancaster.

The **Yorkists** were supporters of Richard, Duke of York (1411–60) and his son, Edward, who became King Edward IV.

Richard, Duke of York was Henry VI's cousin. He always swore loyalty to Henry until, in 1460, he said that he had a better claim to the crown than Henry. When Richard was killed at the battle of Wakefield (1460) his son, Edward, became Yorkist leader. He was crowned King Edward IV in 1461.

DECLINE

5. 1455–59 A phoney peace
There were no more battles for four years. Nearly all the nobles wanted peace and to stay loyal to Henry VI despite his failures. However, in 1459 war broke out because of distrust between the leaders.

4. 1455 The first battle
The first battle was a fight between the Dukes of Somerset and York over who should be King Henry's chief councillor. York won and Somerset was killed. Everyone hoped that this would be the only battle and they could rebuild England as a strong, united country.

6. 1459–61 The fight for the crown
The Lancastrians (supporters of Henry VI) feared that York wanted to depose Henry. York feared that the Lancastrians would attack him. Their mutual fears led them to build up armies and six battles were fought in 18 months. York was killed but his son, Edward, won the battle of Towton, deposed Henry and became King Edward IV. Henry and Margaret fled to Scotland. This was the period of greatest violence – England had sunk a long way from the successes of Henry V.

FAILURE

DANGER OF ATTACK FROM FRANCE AND SCOTLAND

HIGH LEVELS OF CRIME AND DISORDER

The Wars of the Roses: an outline, 1461–85

Essentials 1461–85

1. Twice Edward IV made England more peaceful – in the 1460s and the 1470s.

2. Twice England plunged back into warfare (in 1469–71 and 1483–85) because of the actions of a small number of individuals.

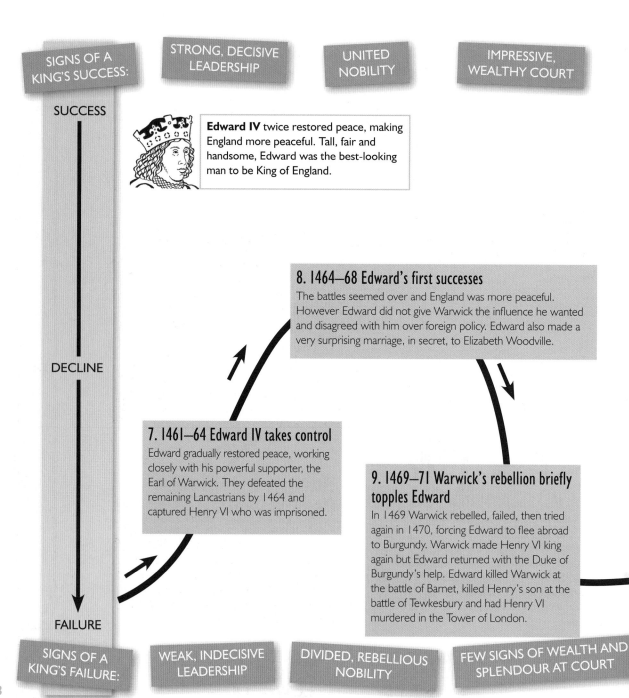

SIGNS OF A KING'S SUCCESS:

STRONG, DECISIVE LEADERSHIP

UNITED NOBILITY

IMPRESSIVE, WEALTHY COURT

SUCCESS

Edward IV twice restored peace, making England more peaceful. Tall, fair and handsome, Edward was the best-looking man to be King of England.

DECLINE

8. 1464–68 Edward's first successes

The battles seemed over and England was more peaceful. However Edward did not give Warwick the influence he wanted and disagreed with him over foreign policy. Edward also made a very surprising marriage, in secret, to Elizabeth Woodville.

7. 1461–64 Edward IV takes control

Edward gradually restored peace, working closely with his powerful supporter, the Earl of Warwick. They defeated the remaining Lancastrians by 1464 and captured Henry VI who was imprisoned.

9. 1469–71 Warwick's rebellion briefly topples Edward

In 1469 Warwick rebelled, failed, then tried again in 1470, forcing Edward to flee abroad to Burgundy. Warwick made Henry VI king again but Edward returned with the Duke of Burgundy's help. Edward killed Warwick at the battle of Barnet, killed Henry's son at the battle of Tewkesbury and had Henry VI murdered in the Tower of London.

FAILURE

SIGNS OF A KING'S FAILURE:

WEAK, INDECISIVE LEADERSHIP

DIVIDED, REBELLIOUS NOBILITY

FEW SIGNS OF WEALTH AND SPLENDOUR AT COURT

3. Almost everyone, including the nobles, wanted an end to violence and civil war.
4. The periods of fighting were quite short but they created great uncertainty and made further rebellions more likely.

STRONG DEFENCE AGAINST FRANCE AND SCOTLAND

LOW LEVELS OF CRIME AND DISORDER

SUCCESS

Richard III was the younger brother of Edward IV. Until 1483 he was loyal to Edward so everyone was shocked when he deposed young Edward V in 1483 and became king himself.

10. 1471–83 Edward IV's next successes
Again Edward made England more peaceful and again people thought the battles were over.

11. 1483 Richard III becomes king; Edward V disappears
Edward IV died suddenly in 1483. His 13-year-old son became King Edward V. To everyone's surprise, young Edward's uncle Richard seized the crown and became King Richard III. Edward vanished.

DECLINE

King for only three months in 1483, **Edward V** and his brother, the 'Princes in the Tower', then disappeared.

Henry VII (Henry Tudor) had no chance of becoming king until Richard III deposed young Edward V. Many Englishmen now distrusted Richard and wanted to depose him. They chose Henry as their leader because he was distantly related to Henry VI. No one knew much about him as he'd lived abroad since childhood.

12. 1483–85 Richard III killed at Bosworth
Richard's seizure of the crown created enemies. One rebellion failed in 1483 but the rebels fled to Brittany to join Henry Tudor who was now Richard's rival for the crown. In August 1485 Henry Tudor invaded England and killed Richard III at the battle of Bosworth. Now it was Henry's turn to try to restore England to the success of Henry V's reign 70 years earlier.

FAILURE

DANGER OF ATTACK FROM FRANCE AND SCOTLAND

HIGH LEVELS OF CRIME AND DISORDER

History on the move: why are the Wars of the Roses so fascinating?

Occasionally I make the mistake of telling people I write history books. It's a mistake because people usually reply, 'Why? There can't be anything new to say. History doesn't change.' If that's what you think then you're in for an enjoyable surprise! As you read this book you'll regularly find examples of historians challenging old ideas and putting forward new interpretations. This page gives you an overview of the major changes in the **historiography** of the wars.

In the 1870s J.R. Green wrote of the Wars of the Roses: 'There are few periods from which we turn with such weariness and disgust.' Green and other Victorian historians saw the Wars of the Roses as a time of complete lawlessness when nobles, motivated by greed and lust for power, hired bands of thugs to destroy kings. Battles, these historians said, destroyed villages and towns and led to countless deaths, all because the medieval system of monarchy had failed. They believed that the Tudors ended the wars by introducing a stronger system of monarchy in 1485.

That view of the wars is long out of date. Interpretations began to change because historians did what they're supposed to do – ask questions. Asking good questions is one of the most important and valuable historical skills. Historians began asking, 'Were the Wars of the Roses really like that?' In the 1920s C.L. Kingsford suggested that the wars had little impact on ordinary people. Then, from the 1940s, K.B. McFarlane set out new interpretations of the wars based on his extensive, painstaking research into a wide range of historical records. McFarlane argued that:

- The problems were created by poor individual kings, especially Henry VI, and not by the failure of the system of government. England did not need a new, stronger monarchy. It needed good kings.
- Many nobles were capable, thoughtful and influenced by chivalric values. They were concerned with the good of the country as well as their own good.
- This was a time of growing wealth and achievement. War wasn't wanted and was slow to develop. There was no widespread destruction.
- The year 1485 was not a new start with the Tudors. Instead there was great continuity before and after 1485.

McFarlane also focused on the periods of peace, asking not just why war broke out in 1455 or 1459 but why war was so slow to start in 1455 and why it took so long to begin again later. McFarlane's work revolutionised thinking about the Wars of the Roses. More historians followed, turning the fifteenth century into one of the liveliest research areas instead of the neglected period it had been. McFarlane's followers explored the careers of individual lords and the patterns of their family connections in their counties – the political relationships between people. This research built a fuller, more sophisticated understanding of the Wars of the Roses.

However, since the 1980s historians such as Professor Christine Carpenter and Dr John Watts have been asking new questions.

historiography
The history of what historians have said about a historical topic

J.R. Green's *A Short History of the English People* was a 'best-seller'

These historians have examined fifteenth century people's thinking about the way England should be governed and about how people should behave politically. This research has developed more complex explanations for the behaviour of nobles and gentry, treating them as responsible, intelligent people. Victorian historians saw nobles as motivated by greed and ambition whereas historians today argue that many nobles took their decisions for more principled reasons. Yes, they were influenced by their own interests but also by the good of the country, by public pressures and values and by public expectations of how the country should be governed. This in turn has led to research into the influence of the common people, especially in towns, and how they saw politics.

So, our understanding of the past doesn't stand still – it's always on the move. It's vital for you to understand that the study of History is **a continuing conversation between historians**. What we know and understand is the result of that developing 'conversation' (even if it takes place in books and articles, not in speech). Each generation of historians builds on the work of previous historians, challenging but also deepening previous understanding. That's one major reason why the Wars of the Roses are so fascinating – there's always new knowledge and understandings to think about.

So, what key ideas should you have in your mind as you begin to study the Wars of the Roses? Here are three important ideas that are the product of recent research:

1. **There <u>was not</u> constant warfare from 1455 to the 1480s.** Battles took place at intervals over a period of 30 years, sometimes many years apart.

2. **Nobles <u>were not</u> constantly plotting rebellions; they wanted a strong, successful king to give them a stable, peaceful country**. Peace and stability were to the advantage of the nobles. Peace meant they could enjoy their wealth. If they charged into civil war they put their wealth and lives at risk.

3. **Loyalty <u>was</u> one of the most important ideals in the 1400s.** The nobles and gentry prided themselves on their loyalty to their king and did not swap sides easily and frequently. This is vital in helping us understand why people were reluctant, not eager, to fight.

These three ideas show the importance of respecting the people of the Wars of the Roses. They were not 'as thick as their armour', ever-eager to ride into battle. Far from it; they did not welcome war, tried hard to avoid it and when it broke out they wanted it to end as soon as possible. Yet war did break out and kings were deposed. This paradox has led to the central question running through this book, a question about people's decisions and why events turn out in ways people do not intend: **if loyalty was so important and people did not want civil war, why did the Wars of the Roses – with all the battles and changes of king – take place at all?**

One more point about History is vital to remember if you are to enjoy and understand your study of the Wars of the Roses. History is the story of real individuals, people who weren't just involved in battles and politics but who laughed and sang, told jokes and fell in love. If, by chance, we had been born 600 years ago, we'd have been facing the decisions they confronted. The Wars affected these individual people in all kinds of ways. Anne Herbert, whom you met on pages 4 and 5, is just one example amongst thousands.

Nobles and gentry: what did they do?

This book has already mentioned 'nobles' without explaining who they were. You know roughly what the word means but to understand the Wars of the Roses you need to know more precisely who the nobility were and what their role was. You also need to know more about another group of people, the gentry, who played an important part in government, and about an idea that was very important to both groups, that of 'service'.

Nobles had one of the titles shown on the right. There were around 60 nobles, the wealthiest landowners, who had land in several parts of the country. They were expected to be the king's leading advisers, to deal with serious outbreaks of crime and disorder and to be his leading commanders, bringing their men to fight in wartime. Nobles expected to do these tasks as signs of their importance. They could resent being left out of such tasks by a king.

Gentry were the next layer down in society. Many were knights so had the title 'Sir'. There were about 3000 gentry families, less wealthy than the nobles, but many still owned land in several counties. Local government was organised county by county and the king depended on the gentry to keep government running effectively in each county. The gentry acted as judges in courts and held posts such as county sheriff. Most welcomed these tasks as a sign of their local importance.

> **Moving up from gentry to nobility**
>
> A good example of promotion comes from the Herbert and Devereux families you met on pages 4–5. They were gentry families but in 1461 they joined the nobility when Edward IV made Sir William Herbert Lord Herbert and Sir Walter Devereux Lord Ferrers as rewards for their support.

'If you've got it, flaunt it!'

Nowadays people can resent the rich parading their wealth but the opposite was true in the 1400s. The king was expected to put on a great display of wealth and grandeur to show off England's wealth and power – a king who looked poor looked powerless. The same was true of nobles. They were expected to show off their riches by wearing fashionable, expensive clothes, building grand homes and having lots of servants. The *Great Chronicle of London* described how the Earl of Warwick was very popular with the common people in the 1460s:

> The earl was ever in great favour with the commons of this land because of the exceeding household that he daily kept wherever he stayed. When he came to London he held such a household that 6 oxen were eaten at breakfast and every tavern was full of his meat for whoever had acquaintance in the earl's household should have as much roast meat as he might carry away on a long dagger.

Clearly Warwick was not being condemned for showing off or mocked as a soft touch. He was being praised for his generosity and as a model for how all noblemen should behave.

Hierarchy of titles

Duke
(mostly royal family)
↓
Marquis
(a rare and new title)
↓
Earl
↓
Lord

Other words for 'nobles'

magnates
Word often used for the most powerful nobles, the dukes and earls

barons
Another term for 'nobles'

The idea of service

People were proud to serve a great lord. 'Service' was one of the most important ideas in the 1400s. Nobles were served their food or helped to dress by young men from other noble or gentry families. These men saw serving their lord as an honour and were proud to be seen as the lord's servants. In return the lord (whether he was the king, a nobleman or a gentleman) believed it was his duty to provide 'good lordship' for his servants, helping them do well and protecting them and their property against rivals. The panel below shows how the idea of 'service' worked.

◁ Members of an affinity wore their lord's badge and clothes in his livery colours. This man wears the white boar badge of Richard, Duke of Gloucester (Richard III) and his colours of blue and murrey (a shade of red). Badges were made of cloth or pewter, a cheap metal alloy. Occasionally lords gave badges of silver to their most trusted followers.

How did 'service' work?

The **duke** has lower-ranking nobles and gentry as members of his **affinity**. They act as his councillors, advising on politics and managing his lands. Some of the local gentry are his lawyers and managers of his estates. They wear his badge and **livery** colours. Many will fight for him if needed. The size and quality of the duke's affinity increases his prestige. His record as a 'good lord' attracts others to join him.

The members of the duke's affinity gain prestige and security by being part of a great man's affinity. They earn money working for him and he rewards them with lands and gifts. He may help them in legal disputes and help them to good marriages by recommending them to fathers of possible brides. They will be grateful to the duke for his 'good lordship'.

A **lord** has the same kind of affinity as a duke but fewer members. He uses them in similar ways, to help run his estates and provide advice and they wear his badge. Men want to serve this lord because he's well connected to the duke, but if the lord loses influence with the duke then men may not be keen to serve him.

The members of the lord's affinity receive the same kinds of good lordship as the duke's followers, but not such rich rewards and prestige. The lord can also protect them but not against the power of a duke.

Gentlemen also have a small group of advisers who help run their estates, sometimes clever young men from poor backgrounds. Gentlemen are expected to provide good lordship to these servants and gain a good reputation by doing so.

affinity
The followers of a lord, men who served him whenever needed or worked for him as lawyers or estate managers. They wore their lord's badge to display their allegiance

livery
The badge and colours of a lord worn by his servants

lord
Lord, with a capital L, is a title, e.g. Lord Ferrers, but 'lord' describes anyone who provides **patronage**, so a duke was described as a man's lord

patronage
A lord provided patronage by giving rewards (jobs, money, influence, titles) to his supporters and protecting them (in court or by force) from rivals after their land or property

13

How to be an effective king

Henry VI became king at just nine months old. He was expected to take control and rule as king from his mid-teens. This page summarises the things young Henry had to understand about ruling England. It's written in a different style, as if giving advice to the young king. Why? To help you concentrate, because it can be very tempting to skip 'background information' pages. This information is really important for understanding the Wars of the Roses, so please don't skip it. You do need to know:

- what a king was expected to do
- what kinds of support he received from nobles, gentry and officials
- the resources he did NOT have compared with modern governments.

As king: what you are expected to do

You need to be a good 'man-manager', uniting your nobility behind you. Concentrate on three things:

- consult your leading noblemen but make all the important decisions yourself
- lead your army in war, providing inspirational leadership
- punish law-breakers severely, make fair judgements, show no mercy to traitors.

Remember, in theory you can do whatever you wish but in practice you are limited by expectations of what a king should do. You must follow tradition and custom, not innovate or change the role of king.

The royal household

The royal household consists of the people who look after you wherever you travel. They range from commoners who work in the kitchens (you'll hardly ever see them) to the noblemen and gentry who are your closest companions and organise your household. They attend you from waking to sleeping, including helping you wash and dress. They also keep you informed about what's happening in the counties where they have land and make sure your orders are carried out there. Reward them well for their service but don't give them so much land that you make yourself poor or look overly influenced by them.

The royal court

The court and the household overlap a great deal. The court is not a place but a group of people: you as king, and your courtiers. Courtiers are there to entertain you with music, chess, gossip, hunting, dancing, maybe a little light flirting. Remember to display English wealth and power through the magnificence of your dress, buildings and court, especially when you greet foreign visitors.

Royal officials

You are supported by around 250 highly trained, educated officials, grouped into departments of which the two main ones are:

- Chancery (headed by the Chancellor) which sends out your letters, commands, grants of land and offices
- Exchequer (headed by the Treasurer) which collects and spends royal income.

This system has been in place for over two hundred years and is very efficient. You'll be amazed at the detailed, meticulous records. They keep copies of everything!

Remember, finance isn't as important now as it will be later in history. A king can be successful without having lots of money in his treasury. Merchants and foreign banks are always keen to lend you money. Just don't get into too much debt or tax your people too often or too heavily. That is unpopular!

The Council

The Council contains the men you choose as your advisers and the heads of government departments, such as the Chancellor and the Treasurer. The Council's role is to make government work and make sure your decisions are put into action. Council meetings (they can be dull) are usually chaired by the Chancellor but you must lead the most important discussions such as decisions about war. Councillors come from the nobles, gentry and bishops (who are often appointed as bishops from among the senior government officials). There can be up to 50 councillors at any one time but only a handful attend most meetings.

Parliament

Parliament meets only when you summon it and closes when you wish it to close – it rarely lasts longer than six weeks. You won't need to call a Parliament every year and you can go for several years without a Parliament if you're not fighting wars. Parliament consists of two Houses: the Lords and the Commons, which includes knights and wealthy merchants. The Lords are more influential but you do have to listen to the Commons. They are the people you have to persuade to agree to taxation, usually to pay for war and defence. You'll soon learn there are times to charm them and times to intimidate them.

If there are problems (war going badly, gentry or nobles breaking laws in their counties) the House of Commons will complain to you on behalf of the commons, the ordinary, very common people. The common people aren't stupid and they're usually well informed, so don't think they can be ignored.

Local government: how you as king control each county

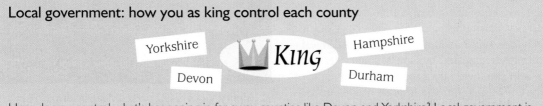

Yorkshire   KING   Hampshire
Devon   Durham

How do you control what's happening in far away counties like Devon and Yorkshire? Local government is organised by county. The nobles and gentry who own land in each county play a crucial part in making local government work. They are the judges in county law courts and if there's a rebellion or major crime they take the lead in stopping it. You must choose one of them as Sheriff, your senior representative, whose job it is to oversee law courts, arrest major criminals and undertake other vitals tasks. You must select the right people as officials. If there's really serious law-breaking you have to go to the area and be seen to deal with it yourself.

Remember, these county communities don't like strangers from other areas getting involved in their local business, so take care whom you appoint as local officials.

As king: what you do NOT have

- A full-time royal army. You depend on nobles and gentry bringing their men to form your royal army
- A full-time police force. Catching criminals is the work of county sheriffs and local constables who are unpaid, part-time officials in each community
- Annual taxation on people's incomes. Your income as king (to pay for your family costs and the royal household) comes mostly from rents from your own lands and customs duties on imports and exports
- Speedy communications. It takes five days for an urgent message to reach York from London

As king: what NOT to do

- Do NOT lose wars against France or Scotland (though it's better to fight bravely and lose than not to fight at all)
- Do NOT ignore high-born noble advisers. Listen to their advice but take the decisions yourself
- Do NOT appear lenient to criminals, especially anyone charged with treason

Henry V and the legacy of Agincourt

The timeline graph on pages 6–9 begins with Henry V, even though he died thirty years before the Wars of the Roses began, so why include him? The answer is that Henry's victory at Agincourt and his conquest of France had an immense impact on the rest of the fifteenth century. To understand later events you have to understand Henry's achievements and the problems they created for his successors.

The conquest of France began with the miraculous victory at Agincourt on 25 October 1415. Henry had invaded France in August, then took a month to capture the port of Harfleur. By then 2000 of Henry's 9000 soldiers had died, most from disease. Many others were ill with dysentery. But instead of sailing home, Henry led his army out of Harfleur on 8 October, heading for Calais. His cross-country march was a display of disdain for the French and quite possibly designed to provoke a battle. If so, he succeeded!

Henry's army had food for eight days but the march took twice as long. The English trudged on, hungry, exhausted by illness, soaked by heavy rain, and shadowed by a much larger French army. On 24 October the English made camp at Agincourt and confessed their sins to God, expecting to die next day. Laughter floated across from the enemy camp where the French were gambling over the English prisoners they'd take in the battle.

Next morning, the day of the Feast of Saints Crispin and Crispinian, King Henry chose a narrow battle line with woodland either side so the French could not encircle his army. He set out a line of knights interspersed with archers but, when the French did not attack, Henry moved his men forward and ordered his archers to open fire. Provoked and insulted, the French charged but the ground, boggy after heavy rain, slowed their horses. The English archers, each man loosing ten to twelve arrows a minute, sent 60,000 arrows hammering down every minute onto the French knights.

The arrow-storm destroyed the French belief in an easy victory and, as the armies clashed in hand-to-hand fighting, the narrow battlefield prevented the French making their greater numbers count. French attacks withered and failed.

△ Henry V (1413–22) was a deeply serious man whose life was built round war. At the battle of Agincourt in 1415 he showed excellent generalship and led his men in the fiercest hand-to-hand fighting. At home he showed the same decisive leadership. Summoning two knights whose quarrel had caused deaths among their supporters, Henry told them to sort out their quarrel before he'd finished a plate of oysters, or he'd execute them both. No one doubted he'd keep his word.

Henry V, his knights and his archers had won. We don't know how many men died (maybe 6000 Frenchmen and a few hundred Englishmen) but the exact numbers are less important than the huge difference between them.

Four days later the church bells rang out in London to proclaim the news of Agincourt. Late in November London's streets were filled with cheering crowds as Henry, simply and soberly dressed, rode to St Paul's to give thanks to God for the victory.

The crowds, far less restrained, sang the Agincourt Carol which began:

> Our King went forth to Normandy,
>
> With grace and might of chivalry;
>
> God for him wrought marvelously
>
> Wherefore England may call and cry Deo Gratias:
>
> Deo gratias Anglia redde pro victoria.

Miraculous though Agincourt was, it was only the beginning of Henry's success. Between 1415 and 1420 he led siege after siege, winning control of more and more French territory. The French nobility, morale weakened by Agincourt and divided amongst themselves, could not stop him. In 1420 France agreed to the humiliating Treaty of Troyes, which not only united England and France, through Henry's marriage to Princess Katherine of France, but also stated that Henry or his son would be the next king of France, thus disinheriting the French heir to the throne.

However, only two years later in 1422, Henry V died of dysentery on another campaign in France. He left his 9-month-old heir a legacy that was both an inspiration and a burden, as shown below.

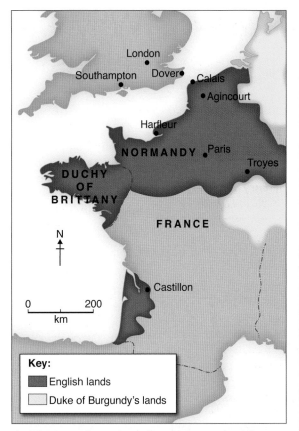

△ This map shows (in red) just how much of France was conquered by the English by 1429. The lands marked in yellow were those of the Duke of Burgundy (see the box below for his importance).

Key:
- English lands
- Duke of Burgundy's lands

Henry V's legacy to Henry VI

The challenge

Henry V had set an inspiring standard of kingship. His successors were expected to match this standard by strengthening English control over France. Losing the lands in France gained under Henry V would be a terrible failure, an insult to those who'd died winning those lands.

The difficulties

Henry V's success had partly been built on an alliance with the Duke of Burgundy and on France's lack of leadership, as the King of France was elderly and insane, believing he was made of glass and would break if anyone touched him. What if Burgundy changed sides to ally with France, leaving England isolated? What if France revived under new leadership? Continued war in France was expensive, requiring heavy taxation: would the English people keep paying if their success ended?

2 Why was London full of rebels in 1450?

Make sure you read pages 16–17 on **Henry V** before you begin this chapter

The graph on pages 6–7 showed that royal success peaked under Henry V around 1420 but that, over the next thirty years, triumph turned to failure. By 1450 England had so many problems that rebels occupied London for several days in protest. By investigating the reasons behind this rebellion this enquiry helps you understand the background to the Wars of the Roses and also Henry VI's abilities as king.

The year 1449 had been terrible for the English. French ships were attacking English coastal towns and trading ships. French soldiers were close to retaking all the lands conquered by Henry V. In Parliament, the Commons savagely criticised the King's chief councillor, William de la Pole, Duke of Suffolk, blaming him for all England's failures. No wonder that the anonymous author of *An English Chronicle* (written in London in the 1460s) noted: 'October 1449, on St Simon and St Jude's day, the sun appeared red as blood. People greatly marvelled, saying it signified some harm to come.' He was right. Far worse did come. The chronicler continued:

In May 1450 the king was **Henry VI, aged 28**

January 1450 – Adam Moleyns, Bishop of Chichester and Keeper of the King's Privy Seal, went to Portsmouth to pay soldiers and shipmen but he tried to cut their wages, arguing with them in boisterous language and they fell on him and cruelly killed him.

May 1450 – The common voice was that the Duke of Suffolk and others had sold Normandy and other English lands to France. At Parliament the Commons accused the Duke of treason and he was arrested and put in the Tower of London. Before this Suffolk had asked an astrologer how he should die. 'A shameful death' answered the astrologer, advising him 'beware of the tower'. The Duke was freed and exiled for five years but when he set sail from Ipswich another ship, the Nicholas of the Tower, lay in wait. They captured him, smote off his head and threw his body onto the beach at Dover.

Cade – although he is called John in this chronicle, other sources and historians refer to him as Jack

And the Kentishmen rose in rebellion and chose them a captain, John Cade, who called himself John Amend-all because the realm had been ruled by untrue counsel so that the common people, because of all the taxes, could not make a living and grouched sore against those that governed the land.

We don't know who Jack Cade was but he was an effective leader. He gathered several thousand followers, using the government's own system for raising soldiers against French attacks. They were summoned by church bells, bringing at least a bow, sword and **jack**. Those bells now rang to call men to join Cade. Messengers, notices on church doors and news spread at Rochester fair also brought men flocking to Cade.

jack
A padded jacket reinforced with metal

Early in June the rebels camped at Blackheath, south of London. The King's advisers sent negotiators to Cade, then an army to frighten him off. Cade led his men away, ambushed pursuers, then returned to Blackheath. The King and his nobles then fled to the Midlands, frightened of their soldiers supporting the rebels. As protest spread, Bishop William Ascough, another of the King's advisers, was murdered in Salisbury.

Cade entered London early in July, riding round, says our chronicler, 'bearing a drawn sword in his hand like a king, wearing gilt spurs, a gilt helmet and a gown of blue velvet as if he were a lord or knight'. Cade now punished men whom the rebels believed were corrupt traitors. The royal Treasurer, Lord Saye, was dragged from the Tower of London, his head cut off and his naked body dragged round London behind a horse. A handful of others were executed and their homes looted. Had the protest turned to random violence? The London chronicles say it had, though some victims were targeted for corruption and Cade hanged a looter. The violence led Londoners to turn against Cade, attacking his men in a night-time battle that raged along London Bridge until the Londoners slammed the city gates, locking out the rebels. Even then there were more negotiations. The rebels were pardoned and perhaps promised their demands would be met. Most went home, leaving Cade and his closest supporters isolated. Cade fled but was caught by the Sheriff of Kent and killed.

Cade's rebellion was a startling outburst of public protest. Why did it take place? Are the answers in the petitions so carefully drafted by the rebels or do we have to look elsewhere?

△ The rebels listed their complaints in petitions to the King, which were also distributed round the south of England. The picture shows most of what was probably the third and last petition. It lists complaints about the King's advisers and defeat in France but the first paragraph is a declaration of loyalty to the King. Cade's followers are usually called 'rebels' but the petitions show they were not rebelling against or criticising King Henry. They repeatedly proclaimed their loyalty to Henry, blaming his advisers for the problems. Most of Cade's followers were respectable; the leaders in their communities. They had a lot to lose, so probably thought carefully before joining Cade.

Chronology of Cade's rebellion, 1450

2 May	Murder of Duke of Suffolk
mid-May	Gathering of rebels
11 June	Rebels at Blackheath, outside London
15–20 June	Negotiations; failed attempt to use military force against rebels; royal army threatened to join rebels
25 June	King Henry and nobles left London
1 July	Cade entered London
3 July	Lord Saye executed
5 July	Battle between Londoners and rebels
12 July	Cade killed

■ Enquiry Focus: Why was London full of rebels in 1450?

How to plan your way through this enquiry

1 Begin by looking carefully at the question. The key word is 'Why?' which means your answer must identify the causes of this rebellion. It will also do one or more of the following:

- explain links between the causes
- identify any causes that are more important than others
- distinguish between the event that triggered the rebellion and the longer term causes behind it.

Identifying these aspects of causation helps you answer the precise question and stops you writing a description of what happened during Cade's rebellion.

2 Now that you have focused on the question you can read pages 21–26, but there's a wrong way and a right way to do this reading!

The wrong way is to start reading and taking notes, pushing the question to the back of your mind. The danger here is that you'll make lots of notes but they probably won't be directed at the question.

The right way is, before reading, to think about the kind of answer that fits the question. You've already read pages 18–19 so what did those pages tell you about why London was full of rebels? For example:

> It says on page 18 that the French were close to retaking English lands in France.

> The chronicle says the Duke of Suffolk and others had sold the English lands to France.

> The rebels blamed the King's closest advisers, the 'untrue counsel'. They executed Lord Saye. Suffolk had already been murdered.

So, stopping and thinking reveals that you already have information that helps create a tentative answer to the question.

Putting together an initial, tentative answer is called 'creating a hypothesis'. For example, a simple hypothesis is:

London was full of rebels because of anger at the loss of lands in France. They blamed the Duke of Suffolk and the rest of the King's advisers for the problems.

Major cause
Suffolk and corrupt advisers

National complaints
Loss of English lands in France

△ This shows the hypothesis in the form of a diagram

The hypothesis gives you a target to have in mind as you read and take notes. As you read, keep thinking. Is new information providing evidence to:

- show that the causes in this hypothesis do explain the rebels' anger
- show that other causes need to be added to the hypothesis
- suggest that some of the hypothesis is wrong and needs changing or taking out
- explain how causes were linked or which causes were most important?

3 Decide now what your hypothesis is. It must explain why London was full of rebels. You may find other information on pages 18–19 to build your hypothesis. Write as detailed an explanation as you can, thinking about the aspects of causation listed higher up the page. Later in the enquiry more blue boxes will prompt you to revise your hypothesis.

The spark that triggered the rebellion?

Why did the rebellion begin when it did, in May, not March or August 1450? The answer is at the beginning of the rebels' first petition:

> Firstly, it is openly said that Kent will be destroyed by a royal army and turned into a wild forest because of the death of the Duke of Suffolk, a death the common people of Kent were not guilty of.

Suffolk died on 2 May, only a fortnight before the rebellion began

The people of Kent clearly believed their homes and farms would be destroyed in revenge for Suffolk's murder. Rumours said that this threat was made by Lord Saye and William Crowmer, the Sheriff of Kent, both close supporters of Suffolk. They'd made this threat after Suffolk's body had been found on the beach in Kent. Saye and Crowmer were extremely powerful, owning a great deal of land in Kent, so it's not surprising that people were frightened. Therefore it was fear of destruction that triggered the rebellion. The diagram (right) shows how this develops our hypothesis.

Major cause
Suffolk and corrupt advisers

National complaints
Loss of English lands in France

Local complaints
Fear of destruction in revenge for Suffolk's death (trigger)

Which other local events created anger?

The threat to destroy Kent was not the only example of the excessive power of lords such as Saye. However the rebels' aim was not to sweep away the nobility nor to depose the King. They simply wanted the existing system of government to work properly and fairly, instead of rewarding a few corrupt noblemen and penalising ordinary people. They accused Saye and Crowmer of being at the centre of corruption among landowners and officials in Kent by:

- fixing elections to Parliament in favour of men they wanted elected
- reducing taxes paid by lords (which had to be made up by ordinary taxpayers)
- extorting money from local people by making them pay fines when falsely accused of crimes.

Given these accusations, it's not surprising that Saye and Crowmer were executed by the rebels in London. Their heads were paraded on spears around the streets as proof that the hated, corrupt royal advisers had been punished.

In addition, a more general reason why so many people joined the protest was fear of hunger and poverty. Farmers and clothworkers made up the majority of the population in the south east and their incomes had fallen. Food prices were low so farmers were earning less for their crops. Cloth sales had slumped (especially abroad) so sheep farmers had less income and clothworkers less work and less pay. Lower incomes meant hunger and poverty, and hungry people are far more likely to rebel than well fed ones.

1 Complete the diagram above, adding other examples of local complaints.

2 Revise your hypothesis to build in what you have learned, using the diagram as a guide. Take time to do this carefully before reading on.

Your hypothesis diagram probably looks similar to this diagram. Pages 22–25 help you develop your hypothesis by looking at the rebels' complaints about national problems. As you read pages 22–25 add notes in the National complaints circle of the diagram.

Major cause
Suffolk and corrupt advisers

National complaints
Loss of English lands in France

Local complaints
Fear of destruction in revenge for Suffolk's death (trigger)

Corruption among local lords and landowners

Fear of poverty and hunger because of trade slump

Which national problems made the rebels angry?

As the rebellion continued the rebels rewrote their petition, focusing less on local complaints in Kent and more on national problems. This was to widen support but also because they believed their protests were for the good of the country and the King. They continually stressed they wanted the King to reign like a 'king royal' and declared they would 'live and die' his loyal subjects. Their target was the punishment of the supporters of the dead Duke of Suffolk, men still in power as royal councillors and in the royal household. They included Lords Saye, Dudley, Beaumont and Sudeley and Bishop Ascough. Those who fell into the rebels' hands were killed. The others would have met the same bloody fate if the rebels had caught them.

The four major charges against these 'false councillors' were that, led by Suffolk, they had:

- **robbed the King and enriched themselves**, taking advantage of his youth and generosity to take royal lands and income for themselves, while leaving the King impoverished
- **hijacked the law courts for their own benefit**, intimidating or bribing judges and juries to make judgments in the favour of them and their supporters
- **prevented nobles closely related to the King from acting as his councillors** and were responsible for the death of the King's uncle, the Duke of Gloucester
- **betrayed England by losing the English empire in France** so that all Henry V's conquests were back in French hands.

What were the details behind the rebels' accusations against the King's advisers?

William de la Pole, Duke of Suffolk (1396–1450)

Suffolk was the dominant politician of the 1440s and the focus of hatred in 1449–50 as England's lands in France were lost. It's tempting to go along with the rebels' view of Suffolk as a 'false traitor', giving away English lands in return for French money, except that Suffolk had a long and respectable career as a soldier in France. Aged 19, he took part in the Agincourt campaign in 1415, fighting alongside his father (killed at Harfleur) and his brother (killed at Agincourt). Suffolk then continued to fight in France until 1430 when he was captured at the battle of Jargeau and held prisoner until he paid a large ransom. Returning to England, he became a member of the royal council from the early 1430s. His fall from power was sudden in 1449, with treason charges leading to his murder in 1450. Cade's rebels thought Suffolk used his influence over the King entirely for his own benefit. Historians have agreed with the rebels but new interpretations suggest that Suffolk may have been less selfish, spending the 1440s trying to do his best for king and country to make up for Henry VI's failings. You'll find out more on historians' views about Suffolk on pages 30–31.

Robbing the King and enriching themselves

Royal income had found its way into the pockets of members of the royal household instead of into the King's treasury. King Henry gave lands to new lords such as Lords Saye and Sudeley, more than was needed to match their new rank. This meant that income from this land went to the lords, not to the King. The Duke of Suffolk was given lands throughout the country but especially in East Anglia and the Thames Valley; Saye built up lands in Kent and Lord Beaumont in Leicestershire and Lincolnshire. Again this meant less income for the King because he no longer held this land. As a result, the King was too poor to pay local communities for food and drink taken for the royal household and ordinary royal servants, such as the washerwomen and stable-hands, went unpaid. By 1448 the crown jewels had to be sold to meet royal debts.

Hijacking the law courts for their own benefit

In 1448 John Paston's manor house in Norfolk was attacked in his absence by a gang of men armed with bows, spears, guns and battering rams. They drove out John's wife and servants and stole his property. Paston was a comparatively wealthy man but all his attempts to take his attackers to court failed because they were protected by the Duke of Suffolk and others who had the power to ensure courts made decisions in their favour. Stories like this were told in many counties. In Kent royal officials collected fines for non-existent crimes or threatened imprisonment to force people to hand over land; they knew that Lord Saye would defend them against complaints.

Preventing nobles closely related to the King from acting as his councillors

People believed that the most important qualification for being one of the king's closest advisers was royal blood, to be closely related to the king. The rebels accused Suffolk and his supporters, who lacked royal blood, of plotting to exclude from power the two men most closely related to King Henry and therefore most qualified to be his advisers – the Dukes of Gloucester and York.

Gloucester was Henry VI's uncle (the last surviving brother of Henry V). The rebels believed Gloucester would have successfully defended Normandy but he had died in 1447 after being arrested and accused of treason. Rumours spread that he'd been murdered on Suffolk's orders to silence his criticism of the lack of war effort. However there is no clear evidence that Gloucester was murdered. York was the King's cousin, a former commander in France. According to the rebels, York had been appointed Lieutenant of Ireland in 1447 to exile him and stop him criticising Suffolk. Again, there is no evidence for this. On the contrary, in the 1440s York had shown no signs of opposing Suffolk's policies.

Betraying England by losing the English empire in France

This was the most serious failure of all. Henry V's successes had left a difficult legacy for his successors: could they hold onto the land he'd conquered? In fact, even after Henry V's death, English forces, led by Henry V's brothers and by nobles who'd fought alongside Henry, won more territory in France. During the 1420s English soldiers settled in northern France, especially Normandy, buying or being granted lands there. Some married French girls; others took their families to live there. Many English children grew to adulthood in Normandy, never having seen England.

▷ Defence of the French empire became harder and harder. English Parliaments were reluctant to pay taxes for a war that was no longer glorious. The noblemen who'd won the campaigns of the 1420s grew older and there was less to attract younger men to take their place. The defensive strategy meant there was less chance of glory or winning wealth through ransoms and captured land.

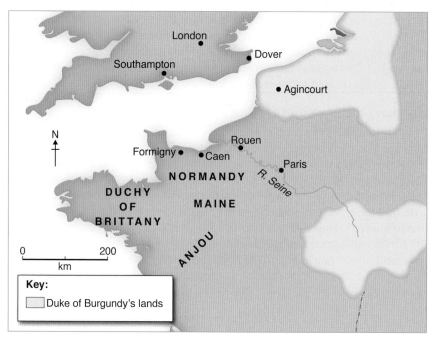

The English survived the French revival led by Joan of Arc in 1429 but the war turned against them in 1435 when the Duke of Burgundy changed sides, allying with France against England. France was also now led effectively by her new king, Charles VII. In contrast, the English received no morale boost from Henry VI when he grew to adulthood. He never led an army to France and, in 1445, when he married the French princess, Margaret of Anjou, he even agreed to give back Maine as a goodwill gesture, a promise of peace.

Despite events moving in France's favour, the sudden loss of Normandy in 1449 came as a horrific shock to the English. French forces tore through a defenceless Normandy, the very core of English possessions. Rouen was surrendered in October 1449. An English relief army landed in Normandy, only to be beaten at the battle of Formigny in April 1450. Caen was surrendered in June 1450. How could this have happened? Simple, said the rebels and the English settlers in Normandy: defeat was caused by treachery. Suffolk and his allies had sold Normandy to the French in return for bribes.

The loss of France shattered national pride. It also had important practical effects in south-east England. Belated attempts to send reinforcements to Normandy, followed by their defeat, had led to:

- soldiers being quartered near the coast while waiting to cross the Channel. Food, drink and lodgings were taken without payment and having so many men crammed together led to disturbances and petty crime
- a slump in the cloth trade because merchants could no longer trade easily with markets in towns in northern France. These towns were no longer in English hands
- an increase in French attacks on the coast. The towns of Rye and Winchelsea in Sussex and Queenborough Castle in Kent were attacked
- a refugee problem, as people who had settled in Normandy now found themselves homeless. One London chronicle recorded, 'they came in great misery and poverty and had to live on hand outs from local people. Many fell to theft and misrule and sore annoyed the common people.'

■ Revise your hypothesis, using the diagram below as a guide. Take time to do this carefully before reading on. Think about:

- links between the local and national complaints

- whether any causes were more important than others

- distinguishing between the event that triggered the rebellion and its longer term causes.

Major cause
Suffolk and corrupt advisers

National complaints
King's wealth taken by advisers
Bribery and threats in the law courts
Leading nobles excluded from advising the King
Loss of English lands in France

Local complaints
Fear of destruction in revenge for Suffolk's death (trigger)
Corruption among local lords and landowners
Fear of poverty and hunger because of trade slump

Why was London full of rebels in 1450? A summary so far

In an early petition the rebels summed up the reasons for their anger:

> The King's false councillors have lost his law, his trade, his common people destroyed, the sea is lost, France is lost, the King himself so placed that he cannot pay for his meat and drink and he owes more than ever any king of England ought, for daily his traitors about him, when anything should come to him by his laws, at once they ask it from him …

Clearly they blamed the King's 'false councillors' for England's problems: for corrupting the legal system, enriching themselves at the King's expense and excluding nobles of royal blood from advising the King. The loss of France was central to their complaints, especially as it had created problems for the people of the south east, who were already suffering from economic problems and from the corruption of local landowners such as Lord Saye. It was Saye's threat to turn Kent into a wasteland in revenge for Suffolk's death that sparked the march to London.

So that was what the rebels believed in 1450, but note that any criticism of the King himself is missing. This isn't surprising. The rebels were very careful about what they wrote. Criticising the King would have frightened off potential supporters. They were desperate to avoid being accused of treason so they regularly declared their loyalty to King Henry and did not criticise him. As a result there is no evidence that the rebels blamed King Henry for England's problems although Londoners, in private, may have complained that his desertion had allowed Cade's rebels into the city (see page 19).

However, historians today can look at the King's role without fearing execution! In fact, we must examine King Henry's responsibility for the rebellion because the King was by far the most important person in government. We have to ask: **was Henry VI the man to blame for London being full of rebels in 1450?**

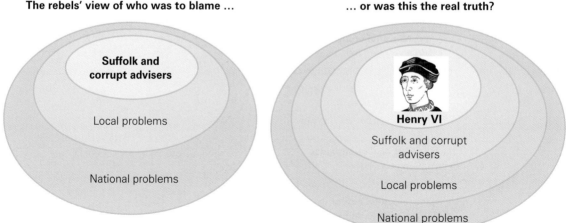

The rebels' view of who was to blame …

- Suffolk and corrupt advisers
- Local problems
- National problems

… or was this the real truth?

- Henry VI
- Suffolk and corrupt advisers
- Local problems
- National problems

The puzzle of Henry VI

It's time for a close-up look at Henry VI who's been in the background throughout this enquiry

In her book *She-Wolves: the women who ruled England before Elizabeth*, the historian Helen Castor includes Henry's wife, Margaret of Anjou, because of Henry's failings as king. Dr Castor uses a variety of words to describe Henry:

gentle; artless; hapless; innocent; unworldly; vagueness; passive; malleable; abstracted

This characterisation is reflected in the portrait shown here. It suggests a religious man: Henry's jewellery is in the shape of a cross, his black cap is simple and undecorated, his hands are clasped gently and calmly as if prayer isn't far away. This portrait was painted after Henry's death, when his successors were campaigning for him to be made a saint, but it chimes with the written evidence which emphasises Henry's religious devotion. Henry's face is also revealing. Compare it with the face of his father, Henry V (see page 16). Henry V looks stern, resolute – a king. Henry VI looks … as if Dr Castor's words suit him extremely well.

This does not sound like a man cut out to be king and this may have been quickly apparent. Professor Anne Curry suggests that when Henry visited France as a 10-year-old in 1431 his guardians were reluctant to let him be seen in public or make speeches in French. Was he slow to learn (despite his French mother) and uninspiring? Henry also complained about noisy shouting in the streets, a rare example of a young boy complaining about a racket rather than causing one!

So what conclusions have historians reached about Henry? Unlike the rebels, they do blame him for England's problems including the rebellion. They agree that he was a disastrous king, but they disagree about the reason. Was he a disaster because he:

a. took the lead and made lots of poor decisions

b. took some decisions (badly) but ignored other important parts of government

c. didn't lead at all, leaving decision-making to others?

Pages 28–31 will help you decide what kind of disaster Henry was!

△ One problem when studying Henry is that, because of his illness and insanity later in life, it's easy to think of him always as an elderly man. But he was only 49 when he died and, in 1450, at the time of Cade's rebellion, he was 28, potentially energetic and active. He was also physically quite strong and sturdy, about 5' 9" (175 cm) tall – not a weakling by any means.

How involved was Henry VI in governing England?

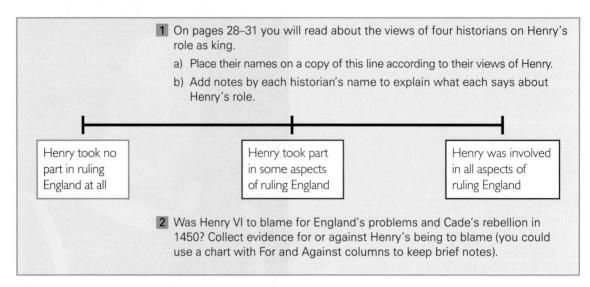

1 On pages 28–31 you will read about the views of four historians on Henry's role as king.

   a) Place their names on a copy of this line according to their views of Henry.

   b) Add notes by each historian's name to explain what each says about Henry's role.

| Henry took no part in ruling England at all | Henry took part in some aspects of ruling England | Henry was involved in all aspects of ruling England |

2 Was Henry VI to blame for England's problems and Cade's rebellion in 1450? Collect evidence for or against Henry's being to blame (you could use a chart with For and Against columns to keep brief notes).

Henry became king in 1422 at 9 months old and was crowned King of France aged 10. Sadly, he didn't rule one country effectively, let alone two, but what role did he actually play in government? Was he fully but incompetently involved, was he involved in some decisions but not others, or was he not involved at all? Let's start with what seem like insults:

> Henry's head was too small for his father's crown.
>
> Henry was inane, … a baby who grew up an imbecile.
>
> In Henry VI second childhood succeeded first without the usual interval.

Begin Activity 1 using the information about McFarlane's views.

These comments seem like insults but they're not. K.B. McFarlane, who wrote them, was a very accurate, perceptive historian, author of many carefully researched, ground-breaking articles between the 1940s and 1960s (see page 10 for more on his work). McFarlane was making a very specific point about Henry VI. Examine his words precisely – 'inane' means silly or senseless, 'imbecile' means mentally weak, idiotic. Put those words together with the observation that Henry went straight from first childhood to second and it's clear that McFarlane believed that Henry always remained childlike, incapable of ruling or making his own decisions. What evidence supports his view?

There's not much evidence of people complaining about Henry but occasional glimpses appear in court records when people were accused of criticising the King. These three comments appear between 1447 and 1449:

> The King looks more like a child than a man. A sheep would be a better emblem on his coins than a ship.
>
> The King is a natural fool.
>
> The King has a child's face and is not steadfast of wit.

Henry VI was in his **20s** in the 1440s

It's tempting to say these comments aren't important because they are few and because they're the views of common people, but where would they have got the idea that Henry was childlike if there weren't some truth in it?

The most detailed description of Henry VI was written by John Blacman who was at one time Henry's chaplain (his personal priest). Here are three extracts from Blacman's *A Compilation of the Meekness and Good Life of King Henry*:

> … at Christmas time a certain great lord brought before him a dance or show of young ladies with bared bosoms who were to dance in that guise before the King, perhaps to prove him or entice his youthful mind. But the King was not blind to it, nor unaware of the devilish wile, and very angrily averted his eyes. Turned his back on them and went out to his chamber …
>
> … the Lord King himself complained to me in his chamber at Eltham, when I was alone there with him employed upon his holy books. There came all at once a knock at the King's door from a certain mighty duke and the King said: 'They do so interrupt me that by day or night I can hardly snatch a moment to be refreshed by reading of any holy teaching without disturbance.'
>
> Once when he was coming down from St Albans to London through Cripplegate, he saw over the gate the quarter of a man on a tall stake, and asked what it was. And when his lords made answer that it was the quarter of a traitor of his, he said 'Take it away. I will not have any Christian man so cruelly handled for my sake.'

Is this useful evidence of Henry's abilities as king? Yes, even though it is not completely objective. When Blacman was writing in the 1480s, Henry was being portrayed as a completely disastrous ruler by the Yorkists who had deposed him. Blacman knew Henry well, respected him and wanted to present him in a better light. Therefore he portrayed Henry as a very devout man, putting his religion before everything else. However, we can infer from this that Blacman had nothing else to praise because Henry had failed as king in traditional ways (as a warrior and firm ruler). The third extract above suggests Henry was simply not cut out for the harsh but vital tasks of kingship. Is there a strong hint here of the childishness other people commented on?

So far the evidence seems to support McFarlane's view of a king who never grew up but in 1981 B.P. Wolffe described a very different Henry. Dr Wolffe discounted Blacman's evidence, saying it was written as part of a campaign to have the King **canonised**; Blacman was too propagandist to be useful. Instead, Wolffe put forward evidence in the royal records, such as: 'Grant for life to William Beauchamp of £100 yearly from income from Norfolk and Suffolk. By the King.'

Henry died in 1471

canonised
Declared a saint

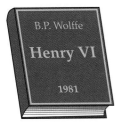

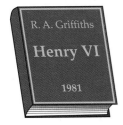

■ Continue Activity 1 on page 28, using the information about Wolffe's and Griffiths' views.

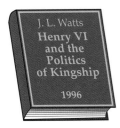

Dr Watts' own explanation of how he developed his arguments is on pages 32–33

■ Complete Activity 1 on page 28, using the information about Watts' views.

Those last three words are the critical ones, suggesting this grant was Henry's decision. There are thousands of such orders in the royal records and Wolffe said these showed that Henry was fully involved in government, making important decisions as a king should. Wolffe believed that Henry directed the peace policy with France and the building of Eton College and King's College, Cambridge. But don't get the impression that Wolffe thought Henry was a good king. He said Henry was a thoroughly poor king, very much to blame for England's problems because he was erratic, sometimes involved, sometimes not, and foolishly over-generous, giving away far too much royal wealth and allowing Suffolk and others to line their pockets. Wolffe's Henry was also vindictive and untrustworthy, plotting the downfall of his uncle, the Duke of Gloucester, and making an enemy of the Duke of York.

This was a very negative picture of Henry but not one of a childlike king. However, also in 1981, Professor R.A. Griffiths painted a much kinder picture of Henry. Griffiths' Henry was a good man, 'not unintelligent', deeply religious and taking some important decisions, such as promoting peace with France. Despite this, Griffiths saw Henry as completely unsuited to be king as he was too merciful to law-breakers and traitors and very poor at choosing advisers. Griffiths' Henry is a sad figure, not the vindictive character described by Wolffe. According to Griffiths, Henry's problem was that he 'never shook off his youthful dependence on others'.

Most historians agreed with Griffiths rather than Wolffe, especially when research showed that Wolffe was wrong to discount Blacman's evidence. Blacman had not written as part of a campaign to have Henry canonised and was less propagandist than Wolffe claimed. Many books you'll find on library shelves follow Griffiths' account of Henry as a religious, naïve, incompetent king involved in some but not all aspects of kingship.

In 1996 came a very different interpretation of Henry from John Watts, who argued that Henry provided no leadership of any kind. He said that records used by Wolffe do not prove that decisions were taken by the King, just that they were taken in the King's name. Watts' interpretation is that Henry completely lacked the willpower to govern and make decisions. In effect he was a hole at the centre of government where there should have been a king providing leadership. Henry's inadequacy was typified by his greeting French ambassadors in 1445: 'he did little more than stand about in a variety of opulent costumes, grinning broadly and crying "Saint Jehan, grant mercis!" when Charles VII's name was mentioned.'

If Henry did not have the intelligence or willpower to lead a government then who was taking the decisions? To answer this question Watts puts forward a second important argument, about the role played by the nobles. Other historians have seen the nobility as simply power-hungry with no interest in the country's welfare. Dr Watts disagrees, saying that Suffolk and others believed they had a duty to act in the country's interests by filling the gap left by Henry at the centre of government. Therefore during the 1440s the nobility chose policies in the national interests. They realised England could not defeat France without an effective king so they took the difficult decision that a truce with France was more in the national interest than war. This much more positive interpretation of Suffolk doesn't mean that he was entirely innocent of blame. He and his supporters still lined their own pockets at the King's expense but Dr Watts argues that their motives were more honourable than previously seen by historians.

So who do we believe about Henry's involvement in government? In concluding this section I can't sit on the fence. My view is that Watts' argument is the strongest. It is supported by contemporary comments and gives the most consistent explanation of Henry's role. To believe Griffiths we'd have to see Henry as sometimes involved and sometimes not, but why would he be so inconsistently involved? Watts' interpretation also makes more sense in the light of people's beliefs in the importance of loyalty to the king and of, for example, Suffolk's lifelong record of royal service. However, not all historians writing since Dr Watts published his research have agreed with him. Some still agree with Griffiths' interpretation and it's likely that these disagreements will continue, so don't be surprised if you read other verdicts on Henry VI in other books.

The paragraph above says, 'I can't sit on the fence. My view …'.

It's unusual to find an obviously personal opinion in textbooks. Normally the writer uses impersonal wording to hide the fact that s/he has made a judgment. The danger then is that the writer's judgment looks as if it's the unchallengeable truth when it's really only an interpretation, though based on evidence and plenty of reading. I have used 'I' here (and elsewhere in the book) to highlight issues where I've made a judgment between competing interpretations.

In this book you'll also see contractions, such as it's instead of 'it is'. This is because contractions make for easier reading, even if you're not supposed to use them in examinations.

Was Henry to blame for the rebellion in 1450?

A summary

One problem with the system of hereditary monarchy – the crown going to the nearest relative of the last monarch – is that the quality of the monarch, like throwing dice, is a matter of luck. England had thrown two sixes when Henry V became king. With Henry VI the dice rolled right off the table and got lost under the floorboards – no score registered at all.

So was Henry to blame? Yes, to a very large extent he was. He never grew into a functioning adult and was completely unable to provide leadership in war or impose justice. One last piece of evidence comes from a Prussian visitor to London in 1450 who described Henry as 'very young and inexperienced', but Henry was 29 in December 1450, a year older than when his father won the battle of Agincourt! How could such a king (whose only swear-word was 'Forsooth and forsooth') frighten the French or intimidate his nobles into keeping the peace?

Should Suffolk share the blame? Perhaps, but only to a small extent. He did build up his power, creating enemies but, once again, the problem lay with Henry's inability to take decisions and settle disputes between nobles. And finally perhaps a little blame lies, ironically, with Henry V whose successes created an impossible legacy for his son. France was almost certain to win back her land but Henry V's successes committed England to a war she would never win.

So, Henry's failures as king were chiefly responsible for the outbreak of Cade's rebellion. If he'd been a successful king there would have been no need for the rebels to protest about everything that had gone wrong. That's why, even when Cade's rebellion was over, the problems remained. Could anyone solve the problems created by Henry's inability to rule?

■ Concluding your enquiry

Finalise your answer to the main question on page 20. Re-read the guidance on page 20 and use the circle diagrams on page 26 to decide on your answer.

Why do historians' interpretations move on?

It's all very well explaining HOW historians' interpretations have changed but WHY do they change? Students sometimes assume that interpretations change only because of new discoveries, of lost documents in a dusty archive, for example. The reality is less dramatic but more interesting. These pages use the example of Henry VI's role in government to explore why new ideas develop. I asked Dr John Watts of the University of Oxford to explain how he developed his interpretations of Henry VI (discussed on pages 30–31). My questions are in red, John's answers in black.

Q What part do you think Henry VI played in ruling?

A Henry played an enormous part in ruling, simply because he was the King. But for government to work properly, a medieval king had to rule actively and with real authority: he had to take tough decisions, lead armies in battle, promote policy in Parliament and see that his orders were implemented. This is where Henry fell down: he signed a lot of state papers, but it was increasingly clear to his subjects – first the great and then the rest – that he wasn't really thinking about what he was doing. Decisions were all too clearly made by Henry's councillors, and that eventually bred distrust and division, since some were better placed to influence the King than others. We can't know why the King was like this – whether he was a fool, a saint, or someone with a mental health problem – but we can be reasonably confident that he failed to exert his will.

Q How did you develop this interpretation?

A I think you can tell that Henry was like this by looking at the pattern of politics in his reign: the willingness of everyone to work with the King (and his willingness to work with them); the long survival of the minority council, when it should have withered away once Henry was in his late teens; the weakness of successive ministers and the ready suspicion that they were bending the King to their will. But if we are going to draw conclusions from what happened, we have to have a sense of what *ought* to have happened, and for me, starting my PhD in 1986, that meant thinking about what the system of government really was in late medieval England.

At that time, historians were paying more attention to noblemen and their affinities in the localities than they were to central government. Most work on the period looked at politics as if it were a private matter – backroom deals between the major players – and most people thought that fifteenth-century political society was highly competitive and unprincipled. In Cambridge, where I was studying, there was a group of historians who were beginning to think differently, notably Ted Powell, Rosemary Horrox and, above all, my supervisor, Christine Carpenter. These historians were arguing that there must be more to politics than patronage, bribery and forcefulness, and that if we wanted to understand what happened in the fifteenth century, we would need to look at politics in a more 'public' way: that is, to consider what people's expectations and beliefs were and also to think about the structures of royal government – the legal system, the king's court and the mechanisms of counsel and petitioning – and the influence they had on the interactions of powerful individuals.

I decided to look at Henry VI's reign in this way, partly because as an undergraduate I'd already done some work on Richard of York, and partly because a reign in which so much went wrong was a good test-case for this

academic treatises
Handbooks written by scholars, setting out how, in principle, the realm should be governed

approach. I focused my research on two main groups of sources. First, I looked at material which could tell us about political ideas (not just **academic treatises** and poems, but speeches, letters and manifestos which could tell us what actual politicians were thinking – or at least what they were saying). Most of these texts were already known, but historical opinion was very dismissive – as if all this was hot air: platitudes and propaganda, not the mainsprings of political behaviour. However, I took a different approach: taking the material seriously, looking for patterns and checking to see whether the things politicians said and did fitted with what was in more highbrow sources – and they did!

The other thing I tried to do was to reconstruct how the inner circles of government worked under Henry VI: how decisions were taken and put into effect, and by whom. What I learned was that Henry's subjects wanted the King to rule, and rule in person; that they saw the exercise of royal will as the best way of upholding the 'common weal' or common good of the realm. Thus, if the King were unable to exercise authority, it must have been for personal reasons – rather as McFarlane [see page 28] had argued many years ago – and not because Henry's subjects were devious or obstructive. This hypothesis was strengthened when I looked at the administrative evidence, which showed Henry's councillors trying to hand over rule to him in the late 1430s, and then finding that they had to manage things for him when he failed to show any initiative or consistency. Throughout the reign, the leading men – and women, like the queen – tried to make Henry's authority work, but they could not: only the King could do that, and his failure to do so explains the breakdown of his government.

Q **Were nobles and gentry motivated by ideals such as service to their country, and how did your views on this topic develop?**

A In a way, I think they were, and this has led some historians (who saw nobles as only self-interested and pragmatic) to accuse me of being naïve, of believing that the nobility were high-minded and altruistic. But this is a misunderstanding of my work. My views were very influenced by the work of certain historians of ideas, especially Quentin Skinner and John Pocock. Very roughly, these historians think political ideas and terms are important because they create the recognised values to which everyone has to pay lip-service. This means that ideas governed almost everyone's behaviour in fifteenth-century politics, both the wicked and the good (and we don't really know who was which at 500 years' distance), because they had to behave in ways that fitted with the expectations of contemporaries. No one had tried to apply this kind of reasoning to the politics of the Wars of the Roses, but it seemed to me that it explained a great deal: the efforts people made to uphold the authority of the king; their attempts to justify themselves by appealing to the notion of the common weal, or their right to give counsel, or the rights of this or that dynasty to hold the throne. They didn't just fight each other: they had to engage in debates, and those debates helped to shape their options and their policies.

How do we know about the Wars of the Roses?

Throughout this book you'll discover that there are many aspects of the Wars of the Roses we're not certain about. So how do we know what we know and why are there gaps and uncertainties? This all depends on our sources.

Chronicles give us our broad outline of events. They tend to be lists of interesting events and incidents written some years after they happened. For example, the chronicles providing the story of the 1450s were written after 1461 and so give a Yorkist version of events. Most chronicles were written in London to be read and enjoyed, so writers often copied chunks from other chronicles that they thought were interesting.

Histories are less random in coverage than chronicles, providing accounts of particular events or themes. The writers were well educated, aware of new ideas about writing history among European scholars. This style of writing was developing from the 1470s. A good example is the continuation of the chronicle at Crowland Abbey, written by an unknown government official who worked in London. This history of the Yorkist kings is one of the most valuable sources for events under Edward IV and Richard III. Edward IV also commissioned detailed histories of the events of 1470–71 (when he lost and regained the crown) to prove the treason of his enemies and to praise his own success.

Royal government records still exist in huge numbers, covering royal council meetings, appointments to jobs in counties, financial records, what happened in Parliament, which lands were given to whom, royal orders to nobles and gentry. Through these records we can follow an individual's career in detail but there's rarely any sense of motive or character.

Newsletters from foreign ambassadors, reporting home with the latest news, provide what are sometimes the most immediate records of events. Their value is often limited by the ambassadors' lack of knowledge of English life, of the background to events or of leading individuals.

Local government records include records of council meetings in a handful of towns. The York city records are especially useful for the career of Richard, Duke of Gloucester (Richard III) and the attitudes towards him in York.

Letters see opposite

Public 'bills'. There was a considerable amount of propaganda, documents known as 'bills', nailed up in public to present, say, the views of Richard of York or justifications for Warwick's actions in order to influence and persuade the public. It's easy to be cynical and assume these are 'just lies' but to be effective these documents had to chime in with people's thinking about how England should be ruled, so they tell us about what people expected from their kings and his councillors.

Buildings and objects. Castles, churches, manor houses, statues, floor-tiles, effigies, jewellery, weapons, armour, furniture, pottery, paintings, toys and games, Bibles and the first printed books in England – the list goes on and on!

What's missing? There's almost no direct evidence of individuals' thoughts and opinions, especially those of ordinary people, to help us understand motives or the principles that shaped their actions. There are very few portraits or good likenesses and often no physical descriptions of even the most significant noblemen.

The Paston Letters

Several collections of family letters survive but by far the most important is the Paston letter collection containing over a thousand documents: letters between members of this East Anglian family and from friends, great lords and people they did business with. They are a treasure trove for historians, providing political news, gossip and insights into daily life. Most gentry and noble families probably wrote letters in this quantity but only a handful survive. There are two very readable accounts of the Pastons and their letters: Helen Castor's *Blood and Roses* and Richard Barber's *The Pastons, a family in the Wars of the Roses*. Here are some very brief extracts in modern English to whet your appetite, all taken from longer letters. See pages 45, 49, 54 and 133 for other Paston extracts.

Margaret Paston on her pregnancy, 1441

Right reverend and worshipful husband … I have grown so fat that no belt or girdle that I have will go round me … Please wear the ring with the image of St Margaret that I sent you as a keepsake until you come home. You have left me such a keep-sake as makes me think of you both day and night when I want to sleep … The Holy Trinity have you in their keeping. Written at Oxnead in very great haste on the Thursday before St Thomas' day.

The battle of St Albans, 1455

… the news we have here is that three lords are dead: the Duke of Somerset, the Earl of Northumberland and Lord Clifford; as for any other well-known men I know of none except Watton of Cambridgeshire. As for the other lords, many of them are hurt …

Gossip

Heydon's wife had her child on St Peter's day. I have heard since that her husband wants nothing to do with her nor with the child she has just had either. I heard it said that he said that if she came into his presence to make her excuse, he would cut off her nose so that everyone knew what she was …

A shopping list, 1448

Right worshipful husband, I commend myself to you and ask you to get some crossbows, and windlasses to wind them with, and crossbow bolts, for your houses are so low that no one can shoot out of them with a long bow … and also get two or three short poll-axes to keep indoors and as many leather jackets as you can … Please be so kind as to buy me a pound of almonds, a pound of sugar and buy some frieze-cloth to make gowns for your children … [and] a yard of black broadcloth for a hood for me …

Queen Margaret in town, 1453

As for news, the queen came into the town last Tuesday afternoon and stayed until 3 o'clock Thursday afternoon. She sent to summon my cousin Elizabeth Clere to her … When she entered the queen's presence, the queen made much of her … Please spend some money on me for Whitsun so that I may have a necklace. When the queen was here, I borrowed my cousin Elizabeth Clere's things because I was too ashamed to appear in beads among so many pretty ladies …

A quiet Christmas

I sent your eldest son to Lady Morley to find out what entertainment was put on in her house the Christmas after the death of her husband. And she said there were no disguisings or harping or lute-playing or singing and no noisy amusements, but backgammon, chess and cards …

3 Why did fighting break out in 1455?

Cade's rebellion had ended but England's major problem remained, Henry VI's inability to lead and take decisions. As nobody wanted to solve the problem by deposing Henry, the only alternative was for someone to govern in the King's name, as Suffolk had in the 1440s. In 1450 two men, the Dukes of York and Somerset, stepped forward as contenders but, instead of working together, they became rivals. Even so, it was far from inevitable that their rivalry would lead to fighting, but it did in 1455. This enquiry investigates why warfare broke out, beginning with an outline of events and an introduction to York and Somerset.

For clarity we can divide the events of 1450–55 into three phases.

Phase 1: 1450–53, Somerset's success

commons
The ordinary people

After Cade's rebellion, Somerset became the King's leading councillor. York made two attempts to replace him. The first, late in 1450, was a political campaign. York had considerable support among the **commons** but the nobles refused to back him because he seemed to be encouraging disruption and disunity so soon after Cade's rebellion had ended. York was politically isolated. Early in 1452 he tried to hit back, marching a small army to challenge Somerset, but backed down because he had little support. Humiliated, he was now even more of a political outcast.

Phase 2: 1453–54, York's comeback

York's main supporters from autumn 1453 were the Nevilles, the family name of the Earls of Salisbury and Warwick who were father and son

Somerset restored order and raised hopes of new successes in France. Then, out of the blue in mid-1453, York was rescued from political isolation when Gascony in France was lost and Henry fell ill, unable to communicate or respond for nearly 18 months. The nobles invited York to join the council and in March 1454 York was appointed Protector, a substitute king while Henry was ill. He had Somerset imprisoned. His Protectorate was partly successful but disrupted by the growth of violent feuds amongst some nobles.

Phase 3: 1455, Somerset restored – conflict!

Henry recovered in December 1454. York's Protectorate ended and Somerset regained power but both men were fearful. Somerset feared York regaining power if Henry collapsed again. York feared Somerset taking action against him. In May, York acted first, gathering an army to challenge Somerset. On 22 May Somerset was killed at the battle of St Albans. York then knelt at the feet of King Henry and begged forgiveness for the violence.

See page 75 for a map of battles

The battle of St Albans was even more shocking than Cade's rebellion. King Henry, a helpless bystander, was wounded in the neck by an arrow. Just as shocking was the breakdown in unity. English nobles were trained to fight the French, not each other. Throughout the 1430s and 1440s they had kept their rivalries in check, putting the King's interests first. So why had those good intentions now fallen apart, leading to English soldiers killing English soldiers in the streets of an English town?

1 Consolidate your understanding of the outline on page 36 by converting
   the text into a time-chart (modelled on pages 6–9) or telling the story aloud
   within a time limit, e.g. one minute. Make the pattern of events clear by
   answering 'How did Somerset's power change between 1450 and 1455?'
2 Does the information on page 36 and below suggest any reasons for the
   outbreak of conflict?

Introducing York and Somerset

When did the rivalry between York and Somerset begin? It's easy to
assume their hostility grew in the 1440s but there's no evidence that it did.
In fact, the two men had a good deal in common in 1450. They both:

- were closely related to the King and had played leading parts in
  government and in France (see page 38 for the royal family tree)
- seem to have supported Suffolk's policies in the 1440s
- had capable, though not outstanding, military records.

York had been Lieutenant of France in 1436–37 and 1440–45 and had won
a reputation for good political leadership while leaving military leadership
to more experienced commanders. In 1447 he was appointed Lieutenant of
Ireland, another important post requiring strong political and military skills.

Somerset had a more distinguished record as a soldier and war-leader
in the 1430s but this was tarnished by being in command in France from
1447 when the English lands were surrendered and lost. With little money
and few resources he'd had little chance of success but, even so, he'd
played his hand badly.

Both men also had 'pasts' but of very different kinds! York's father had
been executed for treason against Henry V in 1415 though York himself
had always shown loyalty to Henry VI. Somerset had had a relationship
with Henry VI's mother, Catherine of Valois, when she was a young widow
in the late 1420s. The Council had intervened and prevented the couple
seeing each other.

Those were the similarities. The most obvious difference was wealth.
York was extremely wealthy with lands throughout England. Somerset had
few lands and therefore little income apart from what came from
government posts.

So there is no evidence for rivalry before 1450, which makes the
development of their hostility the more intriguing! Why were they so certain
they deserved to be at the centre of government? Was either man ambitious
to be king? The royal family tree on the next page suggests some answers.

In 1450 **York was 39,
Somerset about 44**

**Somerset's full
name** was Edmund
Beaufort, Duke of
Somerset; we'll call
him Somerset to avoid
confusion

What did they look like?

Very few contemporary images exist of York and they tell us very little about his
appearance. He may have looked like his youngest son, Richard III, who was
short and dark (see page 104). No portraits exist of Somerset. The lack of
portraits and physical descriptions makes it harder for us to see these men as real
individuals. Whereas many people in the 1450s, especially Londoners, saw York,
Somerset and other lords close at hand, riding or walking through the streets,
today we know what famous people look like but rarely see them close up.

York, Somerset and the royal family tree

Understanding the family tree is important for assessing people's ideas and expectations. The numbered paragraphs on page 39 explain:

- Henry's right to be king
- how closely York and Somerset were related to the King
- why both men expected to be among the King's closest advisers
- whether York or Somerset had hopes of being king.

This tree includes the royal family up to 1453, though it has (yes!) been simplified. Family trees for later years are on pages 78, 81, 95, 109 and 119.

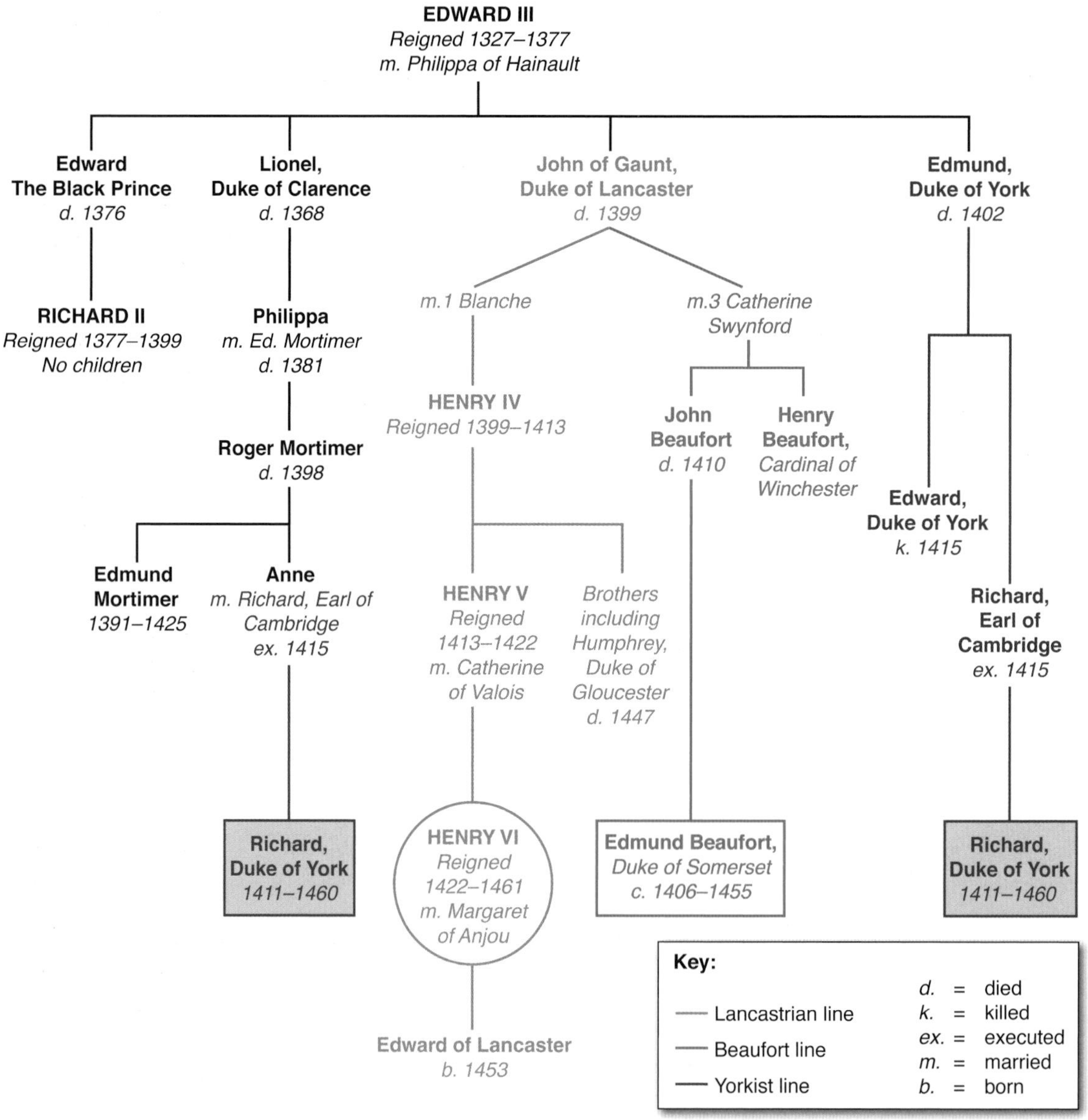

EDWARD III
Reigned 1327–1377
m. Philippa of Hainault

Edward
The Black Prince
d. 1376

Lionel,
Duke of Clarence
d. 1368

John of Gaunt,
Duke of Lancaster
d. 1399

Edmund,
Duke of York
d. 1402

m.1 Blanche

m.3 Catherine Swynford

RICHARD II
Reigned 1377–1399
No children

Philippa
m. Ed. Mortimer
d. 1381

HENRY IV
Reigned 1399–1413

John
Beaufort
d. 1410

Henry
Beaufort,
Cardinal of Winchester

Edward,
Duke of York
k. 1415

Roger Mortimer
d. 1398

Edmund
Mortimer
1391–1425

Anne
m. Richard, Earl of Cambridge
ex. 1415

HENRY V
Reigned 1413–1422
m. Catherine of Valois

Brothers including Humphrey, Duke of Gloucester d. 1447

Richard,
Earl of
Cambridge
ex. 1415

Richard,
Duke of York
1411–1460

HENRY VI
Reigned 1422–1461
m. Margaret of Anjou

Edmund Beaufort,
Duke of Somerset
c. 1406–1455

Richard,
Duke of York
1411–1460

Edward of Lancaster
b. 1453

Key:

—— Lancastrian line	*d.* = died
—— Beaufort line	*k.* = killed
—— Yorkist line	*ex.* = executed
	m. = married
	b. = born

Henry VI's right to be king

1 Henry VI (circled on the family tree) was the third Lancastrian king – 'Lancastrians' because they descended from John, Duke of Lancaster (top, centre right, orange line).

2 In theory, the further someone is to the left of the tree, the stronger their claim to the crown. That was why Richard II (top left) inherited the crown from his grandfather, Edward III. So why did the Lancastrians become kings when there were plenty of people to their left?

3 The answer lies in the failures of Richard II. In 1399 he was deposed by his cousin, Henry (orange line) – Henry IV, the first Lancastrian king.

4 Why was Henry IV king, rather than one of the Clarence line (the family of Edward III's second son), who were to Henry's left on the tree? First, in 1399 there was no adult male in the Clarence line as a rival candidate for the crown. Second, it was Henry who led opposition because Richard II tried to stop his inheriting the dukedom of Lancaster.

5 The Lancastrians were accepted as kings, especially after Henry V's victories over France showed that they had God's support.

Somerset's relationship to the King and right to be a royal councillor

6 Somerset's family name was Beaufort (green line). The Beauforts were closely related to the Lancastrian kings – the first Beauforts were half-brothers to the Lancastrian Henry IV (orange line). They had the same father (John, Duke of Lancaster) but different mothers. The Beauforts were illegitimate, born before John of Lancaster married their mother Catherine.

7 The Beauforts were strong supporters of the Lancastrian kings. In 1450 the senior member of the family was Edmund Beaufort, Duke of Somerset (green box). Somerset expected to be among the King's closest advisers because of his close blood relationship to Henry VI.

York's relationship to the King and right to be a royal councillor

8 Richard of York appears twice on this tree! Follow the blue York line from Edward III's fourth son to find Richard (blue box) – and he's also shown further left in another blue box. That's because his father (the Earl of Cambridge – blue line) married Anne Mortimer, a descendant of the Duke of Clarence (Edward III's second son) and so jumped across the tree!

9 In 1450 York was Henry VI's closest legitimate cousin. York expected be among the King's closest advisers because of his royal blood.

Who was the heir to the throne in 1450?

10 Somerset could not become king. Parliament had barred the Beauforts from inheriting the crown because of their original illegitimacy (point 6).

11 York probably saw himself as heir apparent, the next king if Henry died without children. However, there was no official declaration of this.

Conclusion

12 York and Somerset expected to be among the King's closest advisers because of their royal blood. Both would also object to being ignored or left out.

13 One last point – you might expect York to challenge Henry VI's right to be king because York was descended from Edward III's second son, whereas Henry was descended only from Edward's third son. However, in 1450 this was only a theoretical claim. What mattered more than theory was what was practical and what people had grown used to. Even when York did challenge Henry in 1460, it was wholly because of practical politics – he merely used the theory to justify a decision made for practical reasons. But in 1450 York was loyal to Henry VI.

> Do the family tree and text suggest any reasons for the outbreak of conflict?

These guidelines will help you build your answer as you read through this enquiry.

1 Draw the table below. Make sure you're clear on the differences between the rows.

2 The cards show possible reasons for the outbreak of fighting. Pencil in where you think any of them may go in the table. You could re-read pages 36–37 for ideas.

3 Read pages 40–51. Use the information and the Activity reminders to decide where each card goes in the table. Make sure you make notes to justify your choices.

You may find this easier if you first read pages 40–51 quickly, focusing on events, then re-read them more slowly, focusing on the reasons for conflict.

A. The immediate factors or events that turned the possibility of conflict into a reality

B. The factors that made conflict more likely but still not certain

C. The factors that created the possibility of conflict

1 Henry VI's failure

2 Public opinion

3 Enmity between York and Somerset

4 Henry's illness, 1453–54

5 Feuds between nobles

6 Henry's recovery, late 1454

7 Mutual fear in 1455

Was Henry VI's failure to blame for the fighting?

Cade's rebellion ended early in July 1450. King Henry finally returned to London at the end of July but he was no more involved in government or capable of leadership than he had been before the rebellion. Henry's continuing failure as king is a vital part of the explanation for the fighting in 1455 because it was the factor that led to all the other developments. For example, one of the king's most important duties was to unite his nobility and prevent quarrels escalating into violence. Clearly Henry did not stop Somerset and York's rivalry turning to conflict. When other noble feuds led to local violence only the king could have stopped them but Henry was not capable of doing so. However, Henry's failure did not make conflict certain or even probable. After all, he'd been a failure before 1450 but this hadn't led to his nobles fighting a battle. Even after 1450 it was five years before the rivalry between York and Somerset led to battle. To explain why the possibility of conflict turned to certainty we have to look beyond Henry to other factors.

■ Where would you put Card 1 in the Activity table and why?

Before answering, consider this: I've suggested that Card 1 goes in Row C, even though the text says that Henry's failure was a 'vital part of the explanation for the fighting'. How can something vital be only in Row C?

A. The immediate factors or events that turned the possibility of conflict into a reality

B. The factors that made conflict more likely but still not certain

C. The factors that created the possibility of conflict

1 Henry VI's failure

Events: York's first attempt to win power, 1450–51

York and Somerset were overseas during Cade's rebellion, York in Ireland as King's Lieutenant, Somerset in Normandy where he had surrendered England's lands. Somerset returned first, in August 1450, quickly becoming leader of the royal household and Henry's leading adviser. Why did Somerset take the lead? Although he appears to have been forceful and competent he wasn't taking on an easy task, as stepping into Suffolk's shoes was dangerous given the public hostility to 'evil councillors'. In all likelihood Somerset was driven by a combination of both his own needs and the King's. From his own point of view he needed to be close to the King to ensure a flow of income to match his status as a duke. He wasn't wealthy, despite his title, and had lost significant land and income in France. The King also needed someone to lead his government and Somerset was following his Beaufort family record of loyalty to the Lancastrian kings. Somerset also had support, despite his loss of Normandy, from senior nobles including men with long experience in France, such as England's most famous soldier, John Talbot, Earl of Shrewsbury. They supported him because he was closely related to the King and because they hoped he would restore the government's authority after Cade's rebellion.

York could not return from Ireland until he was sure that there would be no Irish rebellion taking advantage of the problems in England. He finally returned in September, anxious to clear his name of conspiring with Cade and of having his eyes on the crown. Suspicion of him had spread for two reasons: the rebels had proposed York as the man to be the King's leading adviser and Cade had used the alias of Mortimer, the name of York's mother's family who had a claim to the throne. As rumours spread of what York might do on his return, the government's anxiety increased and men from the royal household were sent to meet York when he landed from Ireland. Exactly what their task was is unclear but York claimed they'd been sent to arrest him and that he was being treated as an enemy by Somerset. These events show that even in September 1450 mutual fear was already driving the thinking and actions of both York and Somerset.

As York travelled to the Parliament assembling in London, he exchanged a series of public letters with the King's councillors. These were sophisticated public propaganda, designed to win support amongst commons and lords. York continually emphasised his loyalty to Henry but put forward the argument believed by the commons, that corrupt courtiers (now headed by Somerset) dominated the King and needed to be replaced with a good man closely related to the King (York himself).

Once York arrived in London a mass demonstration called for Somerset to be charged with treason because of his failure in Normandy. Somerset was attacked, leaving York to restore order. Briefly the momentum was with York, thanks to widespread support amongst the people in and around London and in the House of Commons in Parliament. However, at the same time York had alarmed many nobles because they saw his repetition of the rebels' case as creating disunity,

See page 38 for **York's links to the Mortimers** and their place on the royal family tree

Chronology 1450–51

1450

12 July	Death of Cade
August	Somerset returns from Normandy
September	York returns from Ireland, lands in north Wales and travels to East Anglia
November	Parliament opens; York arrives in London

1451

January	Henry, Somerset and nobles hold courts in Kent to punish rebels

possibly increasing the chances of another rebellion. Once Parliament broke up for Christmas, reducing the public clamour for change, the nobility swung behind Somerset. In early 1451 Somerset took the King on progress into Kent, where he executed many of those involved in Cade's rebellion in what was known as 'the harvest of heads'. By then it was clear that Somerset was governing in the King's name with the approval of the nobility. In contrast, York had been excluded from power.

The impact of public opinion

You may be surprised to see the words 'public opinion' when events seem dominated by kings and nobles. However, Cade's rebellion had shown that the commons (from gentry to merchants to tavern-keepers and their customers) were politically aware and had developed their own clear explanation for England's problems. They believed that problems were rooted in the power of corrupt and treacherous courtiers. Although Suffolk and Saye were dead, their former allies were still in the royal household and so there was general fear that little had changed.

People wanted a new beginning and for the King's government to recognise that it had a responsibility to listen to 'the common voice', the wishes and ideals of the common people. Thus, expectation had built up in summer 1450 that York would provide this new beginning by representing the 'common voice' and opposing the royal household, now led by Somerset. In these circumstances York probably had little choice other than to take this role. To turn it down would have placed him, in the eyes of the commons, in the same camp as the 'traitors' around the King. Therefore public opinion gave him support in 1450 but, at the same time, manoeuvred York into becoming the voice of opposition to the royal household and thus Somerset's direct opponent. This opposition ultimately led to St Albans five years later. York's fellow nobles also now believed he was putting personal ambition before national utility.

Where would you place Card 2 on the Activity table? What arguments support your choice?

2

Public opinion

The enmity between York and Somerset

Why did their enmity begin and why couldn't they work together? On page 41 we looked at Somerset's motives for becoming Henry's chief adviser. Once in power, he opposed York because York seemed to be stirring up disunity and because he refused to give up opposition. However, the reasons behind York's hatred of Somerset are less clear. In the past historians suggested that York was driven to become the King's leading councillor by:

See page 37 for the **absence of hostility between York and Somerset** before 1450

- the desire to depose Henry and become king himself, or
- financial need, stemming from the government's failure to pay his debts from his time in command in France.

However, more recent research shows that in 1450 York had no plans to be king and financially had been treated no worse than other noblemen. It is more likely that York was driven by some or all of the following personal motives. We have no way of knowing how important each was.

1. York may well have had a strong sense of duty and destiny. One of the books he owned was a life story of the Roman consul Stilicho, who had been begged by the poor of Rome to restore good government after the failures of the evil councillors of a child-ruler. The parallels with 1450 were clear. 'Mark [take note of] Stilicho's life,' was the translator's message to York and York may have believed he was a Stilicho for the 1450s, the man to put England right, having already been successful in France and Ireland. Thus, his sense of duty and destiny may have combined strongly with the force of public opinion (explained on page 42) to oppose Somerset.

2. York did not rate Somerset's abilities after his failure in France. More personally, York denounced Somerset for surrendering Rouen (Normandy) without fighting. This mattered to York because, though he was in Ireland, he was still absentee commander of Rouen. York said that Somerset's lack of chivalry had besmirched his (York's) own honour.

3. York feared his position as heir apparent was in jeopardy if he were excluded from power. He may have thought that Somerset had his eyes on the crown, though there is no evidence for this. See the family tree on page 38 for York's claim to the throne.

Therefore, by the end of 1450, the two dukes had taken up deeply opposed positions and from then on it was impossible for either to back down. They were already treating each other as enemies, each interpreting the other's actions as an attack, and so each new move ratcheted up the possibility of conflict.

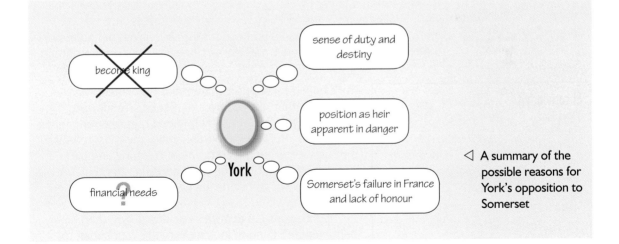

▷ A summary of the possible reasons for York's opposition to Somerset

■ Place Card 3 on the Activity table. What arguments support your choice of position? How might this factor be linked to the role of public opinion and to Henry VI's failure?

3

Enmity between York and Somerset

York's second failure, 1452

See map on page 75 for **places named here**

In May 1451 one of York's supporters, Thomas Young, tried to have York recognised in Parliament as Henry's heir apparent. He failed and his arrest and imprisonment showed how little power York had. However, York had not given up opposition. In September 1451 he paraded his leadership potential when he stepped in to restore peace after the Earl of Devon besieged Lord Bonville in Taunton Castle. York had a right to do this as senior Justice of the Peace in the county but he was also showing he could restore order and settle quarrels.

However, instead of receiving thanks, York was accused of breaking the peace himself and some of his men were harassed by the government. He replied by issuing a declaration of loyalty to Henry but also accusing his 'enemies, adversaries and evil-willers' of making the King distrust him. Then, in February 1452, York gathered his supporters and marched from his castle in Ludlow towards London. He sent out letters to towns and potential supporters, setting out his complaints about Somerset. His letter to the town of Shrewsbury says:

> … after my coming out of Ireland, I, as the King's true liege man (and shall ever be to my life's end), advised his royal majesty concerning the well-being of his person and his realm, which advice was laid aside through the envy, malice and untruth of the Duke of Somerset who labours continually about the King for my undoing, to disinherit me and my heirs. Therefore, with the help of Almighty God and all the company of Heaven, seeing that the Duke rules about the King and that by this means the land is likely to be destroyed, I am determined to take action against him to promote the peace and defence of this land. I will stay loyal to the King and pray you to assist me with as many good and likely men as you can muster and pray that as they travel to meet me they do no robbery or oppression upon the people.

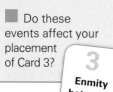

■ Do these events affect your placement of Card 3?

3
Enmity between York and Somerset

York hoped for support in Kent but his armed demonstration turned into a pathetic surrender at Dartford. Only two noblemen joined him, the remainder standing by Somerset. To the nobility the most important aim was restoring the authority of the King and his government, so they stood by Somerset. To them, York again appeared to be stirring up trouble and the danger of rebellion.

Negotiations led to York's backing down, then his being led into London looking very like a prisoner, to swear an oath of loyalty to Henry. York had failed ignominiously but the mutual enmity and fear had increased: York was now even more resentful of Somerset and Somerset knew that York would not admit defeat.

Chronology 1451–52

1451

May	Thomas Young imprisoned for seeking recognition of York as heir apparent
September	York intervenes in Devon–Bonville dispute

1452

February	York confronts Somerset at Dartford but backs down

1453: Defeat in France and Henry's collapse

With York again in political isolation, Somerset steered the government through one of its more successful periods during 1452 and early 1453:

- Henry was taken on progress to punish rebels, including visits to York's lands where men who'd supported York in 1452 were punished.

- The nobility were united in their desire to support Henry and end disorder and fears of rebellion.

- When Parliament met early in 1453 it granted taxes to pay for another military expedition to France, a sign of goodwill and confidence in how Somerset's government was shaping.

In addition, Parliament heard the news that the Queen was pregnant. The birth of a son created a sense of continuity for the future. The only cloud was the development of violent private feuds amongst nobles. Even so, there seemed no way back for York until chance changed his fortunes. In summer 1453 came two pieces of shocking news:

1. Defeat in France at the battle of Castillon. John Talbot, Earl of Shrewsbury, one of the heroes of the wars, was killed. Hopes of success in France were at an end. This was a major blow to the reputation of Somerset's government, raising fears of a French invasion of England. Could Somerset (who had lost Normandy) be trusted to defend England?

2. The King collapsed in August 1453, falling into a kind of coma until Christmas 1454. Although he could be fed and could move he showed no awareness of anything happening around him and could not respond to people talking to him. Henry's collapse was to have profound effects.

> **Titles and places**
>
> A title such as Duke of York did not mean that the duke was based or even owned land in York. Richard, Duke of York's main castles were at Ludlow in Shropshire and Fotheringhay in Northamptonshire. This mismatch of names and areas of power applied to many nobles

---

Henry's illness and treatment

Prince Edward's birth gives us a picture of Henry's illness. In January 1454 a newsletter in the Paston collection says:

> … the Duke of Buckingham took [the Prince] in his arms and presented him to the King, beseeching the King to bless him; and the King gave no kind of answer. The Queen presented him to the King but all their labour was in vain for they received no answer or expression, saving only that once he looked on the Prince and cast his eyes down again.

Doctors followed the Ancient Greek Theory of the Four Humours, believing that people fell ill when the four humours in their body (blood, phlegm, black bile, yellow bile) were out of balance. They also assumed that health was affected by temperament. Henry's December birth gave him a phlegmatic temperament (influenced by the humour phlegm), typified by lack of passion, hatred of violence, and appearing withdrawn, forgetful and pallid with a childlike face. Henry fitted this pattern so well that his collapse can't have surprised his doctors.

Doctors treated Henry by trying to restore the balance of his humours. Treatments included laxatives, sweating in hot baths and bleeding to reduce the excess phlegm causing his illness. Other treatments for jolting a phlegmatic out of his lethargy were talking loudly, pulling his hair and using a feather to make him sneeze. His diet was hot food, such as chicken broth, to counter the cold, watery phlegm.

Chronology 1453–54

1453

March	Parliament granted taxes to pay for an army to invade Gascony in southern France
July	English army defeated at battle of Castillon in Gascony
August	Henry collapsed; attack on Neville wedding party by Percys
October	Birth of Prince Edward; confrontation between Nevilles and Percys in Yorkshire
November	York attended Great Council; Somerset accused of treason and imprisoned

1454

April	York Protector; Salisbury Chancellor
May	Exeter and Egremont rising; Council refused to put Somerset on trial for treason

The impact of Henry's illness, 1453–54

Would the King's recovery be as swift as his collapse? Nobody knew. Government continued but violence was flaring in several areas as a result of feuds between nobles. Somerset could not control it. He didn't have the authority of a king and he dare not take strong action in case any lord he punished turned against him. As a result, a Great Council of nobles was summoned, including York. His involvement was a sign that the nobles were united and committed to restoring the government's authority. He was also the King's nearest adult relative. Although Prince Edward's birth in October meant York was no longer heir apparent, even royal babies were vulnerable to disease and so the possibility of York's becoming king was still strong.

However, despite the general desire for unity, York continued his attack on Somerset when the Council met. The Duke of Norfolk, on York's behalf, demanded Somerset be taken to the Tower and put on trial for treason. No one opposed York, probably because confidence in Somerset's leadership had faded after the defeat in France that summer and the outbreaks of feuds. Somerset was imprisoned but not put on trial. The nobility feared that a trial would create a serious divide, for and against Somerset, that could lead to fighting. However, York was now clearly the central figure in government thanks to Henry's illness, which had transformed the political situation. Until then there had seemed no chance of York challenging Somerset. Even now, however, fighting was not about to break out as York no longer had reason to fight, Somerset was not able to and the nobles did not want it.

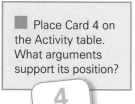

■ Place Card 4 on the Activity table. What arguments support its position?

4

Henry's illness, 1453–54

Queen Margaret and Prince Edward

Margaret was the Duke of Anjou's daughter and niece of the King of France. She married Henry in 1445, aged 15. Their marriage was soon unpopular as she was blamed for England surrendering the county of Maine to France and there was no compensating patter of tiny royal feet. There is no evidence of Margaret's seeking more power than was usual for a queen until Henry's illness and the birth of Prince Edward. She then intervened to safeguard her son's position, though still through negotiation not aggression. Early in 1454 she lobbied to be made Regent with full royal power during Henry's illness but the idea of a queen ruling (and a French queen!) was not acceptable. Margaret remained in the background of events until after the battle of St Albans in 1455. For discussion of Margaret's later role see pages 54–55.

Noble feuds and their impact

During 1453, the absence of effective kingship led to nobles' quarrels over land turning into localised fighting. If there had been an effective king then the quarrelling sides would have appealed to him to adjudicate but, without anyone to decide and enforce that decision, the opposing families used force to settle their arguments.

The powerful Neville family was at the centre of two important feuds. The head of the Nevilles was Richard Neville, Earl of Salisbury, owner of widespread estates in the north and a long-standing supporter of the Lancastrians and Henry VI. His son, also Richard Neville, was Earl of Warwick and had inherited great estates, especially in the Midlands, through his marriage. They had sympathised with York when he returned from Ireland in 1450 but had backed Somerset in 1452 because there was more chance of building royal authority and unity around Somerset. This sometimes surprises students because Salisbury and York were brothers-in-law, but relationship by marriage was so common amongst nobles that it rarely seems to have affected political choices.

> In 1453 **Salisbury was aged 53, Warwick was 25**. Salisbury had three other sons whom we'll meet later

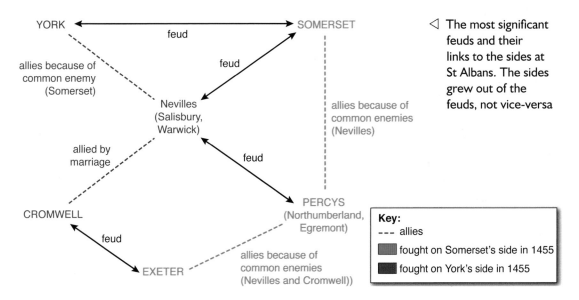

◁ The most significant feuds and their links to the sides at St Albans. The sides grew out of the feuds, not vice-versa

1. Early in 1453 Warwick and Somerset were rival claimants to inherit lands in Glamorgan. Warwick held them but Somerset ordered him to hand them over. Warwick refused, for the first time opening a breach between the Nevilles and Somerset.

2. The Nevilles were in dispute with the Percys (led by the Earl of Northumberland), another major northern family. The Percys were frustrated at the increasing wealth and dominance of the Nevilles and by the Nevilles' poor leadership of a military expedition against Scotland which led to a Percy son being captured and ransomed. However, the immediate cause of violence was a land dispute and marriage! The land at Wressle in Yorkshire had once belonged to the Percys but was now held by Lord Cromwell. The marriage was between Cromwell's heir, Maud Stanhope, and Thomas Neville.

For **Tattershall Castle** and Lord Cromwell see page 52

This meant that one day the Nevilles would inherit Wressle, the former Percy land. The Percys were furious. In August 1453 the Percys (led by their wild, violent younger son, Lord Egremont) attacked the Nevilles at Heworth Moor near York as the Nevilles travelled back from the wedding at Tattershall Castle. The Nevilles fought their way to safety but further violence was inevitable. By October the north was split into two armed camps, Neville and Percy.

3. A further feud developed between Cromwell and Exeter. The Duke of Exeter was one of the few noblemen who made up in thuggery what he lacked in brains. Exeter seized the estate of Ampthill in Bedfordshire from Lord Cromwell. Cromwell tried to get his land back through the law courts but failed, leading to an armed brawl between the men's retainers. Now this is where it gets tricky. To adapt an old saying, 'my enemy's friend's enemy is my friend', Exeter's enemy was Cromwell, whose friends were the Nevilles, and the Nevilles' enemies were the Percys, so Exeter joined the Percys, his enemy's enemy!

My	enemy's	friend's	enemy	is	my friend
Exeter	Cromwell	Nevilles	Percys		Exeter–Percys

York's Protectorate 1454

Across the winter of 1453–54 the nobles discussed how best to restore order and maintain the government's authority. It seems that a group of nobles, led by the Nevilles and Cromwell, argued that York would provide the most effective leadership. By March 1454 this view won general approval, leading to York's being appointed **Protector** while the King was ill. He was supported by a council of 24 men, partly at his request, to share the responsibility. As a declaration of loyalty and to silence suspicions, York swore an oath recognising Prince Edward as heir to the throne and promising the prince would become Protector when he was old enough. Shortly afterwards, the Earl of Salisbury was appointed **Chancellor** after the death of Archbishop Kemp. Salisbury was the first non-churchman to be Chancellor in 50 years but his long experience and loyalty to Henry made him a good choice.

York made great efforts to be successful as Protector. He dealt effectively with a rebellion led by Exeter and Lord Egremont, second son of the Percy family. Exeter resented York's appointment as Protector, believing (wrongly) he had a better right by blood to the role. He planned to assassinate York but York, with Neville support, had Exeter and Egremont imprisoned.

This exemplified York's successes and problems. He had ended a rebellion but it could look as if he were acting only in his own and the Nevilles' interests rather than in the interest of the King and country. He also tried to deal with disputes in Devon, Wales and Derbyshire, summoning the feuding lords to attend him but they simply ignored him.

The impact of feuds

Until 1453 York had been politically isolated. However, during Henry's illness, the majority of the nobles supported him as the man most likely to restore order and royal authority. This was part of the Nevilles' motivation for supporting him but they also saw an advantage for themselves. Once in power, York would give them official support against the Percys. In contrast,

Protector
The official substitute for the king, leading his army, guiding the council

Chancellor
The Chancellor was in charge of the administration, the 'civil service'

Salisbury was head of the **Neville family** and Warwick's father

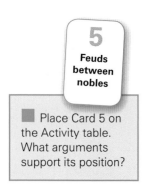

5

Feuds between nobles

Place Card 5 on the Activity table. What arguments support its position?

a handful of nobles, notably Exeter, deeply resented York's sudden power and perhaps saw him as a threat to the Lancastrians. How did these developments affect the likelihood of conflict? The feuds themselves did not lead directly to the battle of St Albans but they did help two sides to emerge. Remember Dartford in 1452: York did not have the support to fight Somerset then but he did in 1455 at St Albans. York's period as Protector and the development of feuds played a large part in York's gaining Neville support and others (Exeter, the Percys) backing Somerset.

Before the King's illness, nobody wanted to ally with York. Why risk being linked to a man who behaves as a traitor?

Now he looks the best man to provide leadership. There's little confidence in Somerset with this recent defeat in France.

And York now has power and authority. He would provide official backing against the Percys.

Salisbury

Warwick

△ The ideas that might have influenced the Neville earls, Salisbury and Warwick, in 1454

The disaster of Henry's recovery

Late in 1454 came the event many had been praying for – Henry recovered. In January 1455 John Paston received a letter proclaiming the good news:

> Blessed be God, the King is well amended and has been since Christmas. The Queen came to him and brought my Lord Prince with her. And then he asked what the Prince's name was and the Queen told him 'Edward' and then he held up his hands and thanked God therefore. And he said he never knew till that time nor understood what was said to him, nor know where he had been while he was sick until now.

In reality Henry's recovery was a disaster, leading to conflict within six months. Somerset was released from the Tower and re-emerged at the centre of government, supported by Exeter and the Percys who were eager to end the influence of York and the Nevilles. Now that the King had recovered, York's Protectorate ended and Salisbury resigned as Chancellor. These changes need not have led to violence, especially if efforts had been made to reconcile the Nevilles to Somerset and the court, but fear and feuds pushed events forward. Both York and Somerset were anxious about what the other might do and both in the end decided to get their retaliation in first.

▽ Mutual fears early in 1455

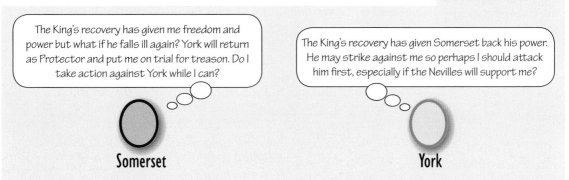

The King's recovery has given me freedom and power but what if he falls ill again? York will return as Protector and put me on trial for treason. Do I take action against York while I can?

The King's recovery has given Somerset back his power. He may strike against me so perhaps I should attack him first, especially if the Nevilles will support me?

Somerset

York

■ Place Cards
6 and 7 on the
Activity table. What
arguments support
their positions?

6

Henry's
recovery,
late 1454

7

Mutual
fear in
1455

Chronology December 1454–May 1455

1454

| December | Henry's recovery |

1455

9 February	York's Protectorate formally ends
March	Somerset restored to power; Salisbury resigns as Chancellor
21 May	Great Council due to meet at Leicester

Somerset took political, not military, action. He called a Great Council at Leicester for 21 May 1455 but did not invite York or the Nevilles. They interpreted this as the first move in having them accused of treason and so decided that the only way to save themselves was with force. Ironically, if this were Somerset's intention, he might not have succeeded. The majority of nobles might have stopped him, just as they'd opposed York's putting Somerset on trial for treason. But York did not wait to find out. Speedily gathering an army, York and the Nevilles marched to intercept Henry and Somerset on their way to Leicester. Somerset was unaware of the possibility of a military clash until 18 May. He then sent messages to nobles, appealing for support, but few had had the chance to arrive by the time both sides met at St Albans, early on the morning of 22 May.

The battle of St Albans, 22 May 1455

Even on the morning of the battle there were hours of negotiations, further evidence of the nobles' desire to avoid fighting. However, with York demanding that Somerset be handed over and put on trial for treason, this confrontation could not end peacefully.

For several reasons we can reconstruct this battle in more detail than most later battles. It was the first battle, a huge shock, and so attracted great attention. Unusually it was fought in a town, so streets and buildings provided landmarks in descriptions. It was also very short, two hours at the most, the fiercest fighting lasting a mere half-hour.

The royal army, 2000 men at most, barricaded itself inside the town. Outside stood the Yorkist army of some 3000 men. In mid-morning York's men attacked but were thrown back. They attacked again, intent on forcing their way into the town, but the outcome was decided by York's allies, the Nevilles. Warwick cut through gardens and the backs of houses to attack the royal army on its flank. This assault broke the defenders' resistance. A few fought on but many ran, most famously the Earl of Wiltshire, disguised as a monk. *Gregory's Chronicle* records that Wiltshire 'fought mainly with his heels for he was afraid of losing his beauty for he was known as the most handsome knight in the land'. We'll see Wiltshire at later battles although only as a distant figure, sprinting away at high speed!

The battle ended with the deaths of Somerset and Northumberland, respectively the enemies of York and the Nevilles. The *English Chronicle* tells how Somerset 'had heard a fantastic prophecy that he should die under a castle and so told the King he would not visit Windsor Castle. But at St Albans there was an inn, The Castle, and outside that inn he was slain.'

More shocking even than the killing of English nobles by their own countrymen was the wounding of King Henry, whose neck had been

In 1455 the fight was
not between York and
Lancaster but between
York and Somerset,
the leading member of
the Beaufort family

grazed by an arrow, and the fact that the Yorkists had dared to attack while the King's standard was flying. As the battle ended, York and the Neville earls of Salisbury and Warwick led Henry into St Albans Abbey. There they knelt in front of the King and begged his forgiveness for the violence. Their quarrel, they said, had been only with Somerset. They were still loyal to King Henry.

Summary: why did fighting break out in 1455?

No one planned to start this conflict until the Yorkists began collecting their army just days before the battle. Somerset and the court party had the battle forced upon them. Thus, this conflict was not inevitable but, by 1455, events had given the mutual enmity and fear such momentum that the battle took place even though the nobles had tried consistently throughout these years to prevent conflict.

Henry's failure, York's support for the public's belief in the guilt of 'evil councillors', and the enmity between York and Somerset initially created the possibility of violence. In 1452 Dartford showed that York had almost no support but, at the same time, Dartford also added to the fear and suspicion. Then came Henry's illness and the latest defeat in France, making York look a better prospect than Somerset for leading an effective government. For the first time since 1450 York now looked an attractive ally for anyone who needed powerful support and the feuds between nobles, especially the Neville–Percy clash, had created that need. At the same time a handful of York's opponents (notably Exeter) resented his new eminence. Then came Henry's recovery. Suddenly Somerset was back, but fearing what York might do. York was an outsider again, fearful of Somerset's revenge. Their mutual fear drove them to take action, to get their retaliation in first. The majority still wanted peace but a small and loud chorus of other voices – the Percys, Exeter, the Nevilles – cheered them on. It was fear of what each other might do that triggered the battle of St Albans.

△ A modern re-enactor shows a longbow's power. Good archers could fire 10–12 arrows a minute over a distance of 275 metres.

■ Concluding your enquiry

By now you should have placed all the factors on the Activity table introduced on page 40. Review where you have placed the cards for the final time and make sure you have collected evidence for each one. You can now use them to write an essay answering our Enquiry question, building each paragraph around one factor. After your introduction begin with paragraphs relating to row C, move on to Row B and finish with factors on Row A.

Warfare or weddings? What were castles for?

It's easy to assume castles were often attacked and besieged during the Wars of the Roses but few castles saw fighting. The only sieges were of the Tower of London, Harlech in Wales, and the north-eastern castles of Bamburgh, Alnwick and Dunstanburgh. Instead, Raglan Castle (opposite) and Tattershall Castle, with its Great Tower (below), were among many castles rebuilt to increase comfort and display power and wealth.

Tattershall did however host a wedding that caused a lot of trouble. In 1453 Maud Stanhope, heiress of Lord Cromwell (the owner of Tattershall Castle) married Thomas Neville. Riding back to the Neville lands in Yorkshire, the wedding party was ambushed! As you read on page 48, this was a key moment in the developing feud between the Neville and Percy families (though what happened to the wedding cake is not recorded).

Who and when?

The Great Tower was built in Lincolnshire in the 1430s by Ralph, Lord Cromwell, a leading soldier and politician. It was one of the first castles in England built in brick, a skill brought by Flemish and German workmen.

See map on page 75

Why?

The tower, with its ground floor entrances and huge windows, was not for defence. Cromwell was showing off his power and wealth in a grand display of building, to impress other nobles and show his supporters that he was a man worth following. The six floors contained comfortable, well-lit living and dining rooms for entertaining visitors. Each floor had its own toilet and fireplaces.

Warfare or weddings?

Tattershall was more suited to weddings. There's no evidence here of fear of civil war, otherwise Cromwell would have built a stronger, more defendable castle.

◁ Raglan Castle was redeveloped between 1435 and 1469 by William ap Thomas and particularly by his son, William Herbert, Earl of Pembroke. The rebuilding focused on comfort and luxury. Family and guest apartments had large, glass-filled windows and tapestries hung on the walls. Food came from the castle's orchards, gardens and deer park. You can see a reconstruction drawing of part of the castle on page 138.

The Herberts of Raglan Castle

On page 5 we introduced Anne Herbert, Countess of Pembroke. Her home was Raglan Castle in Gwent, south Wales. The politics of 1450–61 must have caused Anne continuing anxiety. Her father, Sir Walter Devereux, was one of York's senior councillors. In 1452, while York was marching to Dartford to confront Somerset, Sir Walter stirred up revolts in his home territory of Hereford. For this he was tried for treason but pardoned. Anne's husband, William Herbert, was also a member of York's affinity but even so he was knighted at Christmas 1452 and was made Sheriff of Glamorgan in 1453. Both Anne's father and husband were probably with York at the battle of St Albans in 1455. Anne is likely to have been doubly anxious as it was around this time that her first son was born.

After 1455 Sir Walter and William continued to support York. In 1456 they recaptured Carmarthen Castle for York from Edmund Tudor (Henry VI's half-brother) and attacked the Herefordshire lands of the Earl of Wiltshire, the famously handsome battle escapologist. Arrested and put on trial, Sir Walter was imprisoned but William Herbert was pardoned, perhaps to tempt him over to the Lancastrians. Sir Walter died in 1459 and his lands were taken over by his eldest son (Anne's brother), also called Walter. This Walter was at Ludford Bridge with York, then was **attainted** (see page 59) and lost his lands. He escaped execution after kneeling before Queen Margaret and begging for pardon. William and Walter then fought for Edward of York under the three suns at Mortimer's Cross (see page 60) and in the snow at Towton. Anne must have been overjoyed to hear that they had survived. Victorious, both men were summoned to Parliament in 1461 by Edward IV – as lords!

attainted
Convicted of treason

What colour was Queen Margaret's hair ...

The question of Queen Margaret's hair-colour may seem frivolous and easy to answer. This picture of Margaret receiving a wedding gift shows her with blonde hair. Therefore it's reasonable to assume she had blonde hair, until you discover that all six fifteenth-century English queens were pictured with blonde hair. They can't all have been blonde, so why were they shown like that? The Virgin Mary, Christ's mother, was portrayed with blonde hair and queens were expected to follow Mary as a model; hence Margaret's blonde hair in pictures, her white dress at her coronation and the white horses accompanying her. White, like blonde hair, was the symbol of virginity and all queens were expected to be virgins on marriage and pure in spirit in all their actions.

So was Margaret's hair really blonde? An Italian in London described Margaret to the Duchess of Milan as 'a most handsome woman though somewhat dark and not so beautiful as your Serenity'. So perhaps her hair was dark, although the writer got his description from someone else and was writing to flatter the Duchess, not provide an accurate description of Margaret.

This discussion of hair-colour is a visible example of how attitudes to women in the 1400s affected the way they were portrayed. The rest of this page investigates how new research into attitudes to women is changing our view of Margaret's role in politics. After Somerset's death Margaret emerged to lead the Lancastrians as King Henry was unable to do so. The most common image of her between 1455 and 1461 is as the villain of events, a vindictive warrior-queen, hell-bent on killing York and making all the key decisions for the Lancastrians without concern for people's reactions. This interpretation came largely from chronicles written after 1461, when York's son was king, but it's also summed up in a newsletter in the Paston collection from February 1456:

> The Queen is a great and strong-laboured woman for she spares no pain to sue her things to an intent and conclusion to her power.

54

... and was she really a warrior-queen taking all the decisions?

Even if you can't make sense of every word in that quotation, the letter presents a daunting picture of Margaret as an unstoppable, uncaring force. However, recently Margaret's role has been explored by several historians, including Helen Maurer in her book *Margaret of Anjou: Queenship and Power in Late Medieval England*, published in 2003. Dr Maurer's work is part of a trend in research to explore people's expectations at the time about what was acceptable for women to do, and then to analyse the actions of a woman like Margaret in the context of such expectations. This research suggests that Margaret was not free to do whatever she wanted, as people's attitudes to the role of a queen dictated what she could do.

Dr Maurer's work can be used to explore two crucial questions. First, was Margaret really the warrior-queen, ever desperate to kill York? The answer is 'no'. She worked hard to fit the contemporary ideal of a queen as a mediator and negotiator, seeking peace with York. In the early 1450s Margaret fulfilled this ideal by 'networking' with the Duchesses of York, Somerset and others to prevent violence. Dr Maurer suggests Margaret continued this after 1455. Margaret wanted to stop York from challenging Henry but her first-choice method was through mediation, hoping to bring York into the political fold and prevent him becoming an outsider who might use violence. She supported York and the Nevilles in receiving rewards and important posts in government well into 1458. The climax of this policy was the Loveday ceremony (see page 58), an attempt to reconcile York and Lancaster, a classic example of the pleading for peace expected of women.

The second question is whether Margaret brushed aside Henry and her noble supporters to act as the chief Lancastrian decision-maker, for example in deciding whether to attack London in 1461. Dr Maurer shows how difficult Margaret's situation was: while she was not expected to just sit and sew, she was not expected to step into the King's role as decision-taker. To do so would attract a lot of criticism, but Margaret (like Suffolk and Somerset before her) had no choice as Henry lacked the will-power to take decisions himself. Therefore she tried to fit in with expectations by making decisions in the name of the King or of her son, Prince Edward. She worked with leading noblemen but they certainly took the decisions on the battlefield. For Margaret to be at a battle would have been totally inappropriate. Thus, Margaret did take decisions but, to avoid criticism, was careful how such decisions were presented.

Overall, the work of Helen Maurer and others has similarities with that of John Watts (pages 32–33) by focusing on fifteenth-century ways of thinking and how those ideas and attitudes directed and limited individuals' actions. This is building a much more realistic picture of Margaret than the one-dimensional villainess portrayed in the past. History is moving on!

Other books on the roles of queens, including Margaret, are: J.L. Laynesmith, *The Last Medieval Queens* (2004); H. Castor, *She Wolves: The Women who ruled England before Elizabeth* (2010)

4 Why was Edward IV able to win the crown in 1461?

A critical decision

Lancastrians
- King Henry
- Queen Margaret
- Duke of Somerset (son of Somerset killed at St Albans)

Yorkists
- Richard, Duke of York
- Edward, Earl of March (York's son)

The Nevilles
- Salisbury (father)
- Warwick (son)

The battle of St Albans was over. Henry VI was still king but Somerset was dead, killed by York's soldiers. Queen Margaret emerged as leader of the Lancastrians after Somerset's death. Henry was even less capable than before. Now let's fast-forward nearly six years, to February 1461. Once again, an army is camped around St Albans. This Lancastrian army has just fought the <u>second</u> battle of St Albans. This time they've beaten the Yorkists.

The obvious next step is for them to march south to take control of London. But London's gates are shut because many Londoners do not want the Lancastrian army in the city. Queen Margaret and her advisers face a difficult choice. Should they:

a. advance on London, hoping their appearance forces the city's leaders to open its gates. If the gates are not opened will they risk attacking London?

b. leave London, march north to build an even stronger army and plan one last battle to crush the remaining Yorkists?

This decision was one of the most important of the Wars but before we discover what they decided …

What had happened since the first battle of St Albans?

After 1455 there was no more conflict for four years but there was a lot of fear and suspicion. Margaret feared that York might depose her husband and disinherit her young son. Somerset's sons wanted revenge for their father's death. York and his supporters were afraid that Margaret and her supporters would attack them. In 1459 fighting began. There were five battles in 18 months, ending with the second battle of St Albans in February 1461. By then:

- York and his ally, Salisbury, had been killed
- Edward, Earl of March, York's son, had become the Yorkist leader
- Edward's main supporter, the Earl of Warwick, had been beaten at St Albans and fled.

The only good news for the Yorkists was that Edward had won the battle of Mortimer's Cross (see map on page 75). Edward was marching towards London. Could he succeed where his father had failed and win the crown?

What was Margaret's decision?

What ideas can you suggest at this stage for Edward's success?

Margaret and her advisers had to make their decision quickly. They didn't want to be trapped between Edward's army and London, which might send out soldiers to help Edward. They decided to head back north. Just days later, Edward and Warwick arrived in London. Edward was proclaimed as King Edward IV then headed north in pursuit of the Lancastrians. The two armies met in a snowstorm at Towton in Yorkshire. Edward gained a decisive victory. Margaret and Henry fled to Scotland. Edward had won!

■ **Enquiry Focus:** Why did Edward of York win the crown in 1461? Part 1

This enquiry might be tricky if you try to do two things at once, getting to know the story of events while also working out why Edward was successful. Therefore, it is divided into two parts. Part 1 (pages 58–61) tells the rollercoaster story of what happened, so that you can get the pattern of

events clear in your mind. Part 2 (pages 62–69) explores why Edward won the crown.

In Part 1 the most effective way to record and understand the pattern of events is to annotate a graph. After each section of text on pages 58–61, annotate your copy of this graph to explain its pattern.

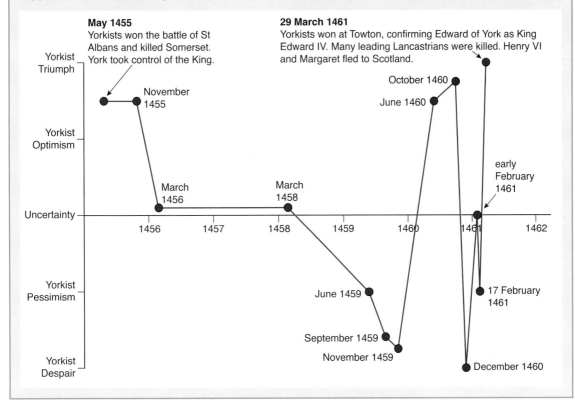

May 1455
Yorkists won the battle of St Albans and killed Somerset. York took control of the King.

29 March 1461
Yorkists won at Towton, confirming Edward of York as King Edward IV. Many leading Lancastrians were killed. Henry VI and Margaret fled to Scotland.

▽ Students sometimes feel confused over the sequence of battles and the pace of events. In what order did the battles happen? This illustration gives you initial letters to make into a mnemonic, such as **S**ix **B**attles, **N**ow **W**e **M**ust **S**urvive **T**owton. Making up your own mnemonic is the best way for you to remember it. You'll understand the pace of events between 1455 and 1461 if you think of their happening while you're at school. The first battle of St Albans in 1455 happened near the end of Year 7 but there were no more battles until early in Year 12 (September 1459), then six more by April of Year 13!

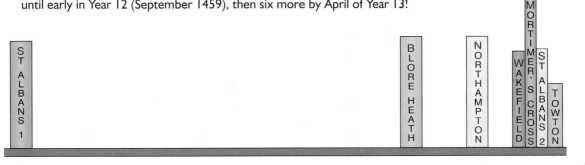

Peace and war 1455–61

Four years of 'peace' 1455–59

Nobody had wanted the quarrel between York and Somerset to lead to battle in 1455. The nobles were loyal to Henry VI and wanted St Albans to be the end of fighting, not the beginning. York and the Nevilles (Salisbury and Warwick) also hoped there'd be no more battles. They'd killed their enemies (Somerset and Northumberland) at St Albans and more fighting would only put their success at risk. York became Protector again in November 1455, ruling on behalf of Henry, and the majority of the nobles accepted York as Protector. Warwick became Captain of Calais (the last English town in France), a powerful position because Calais had its own garrison of soldiers, now under Warwick's command.

However, Queen Margaret did not trust York's loyalty. We don't know her thoughts or the reasons for them but she most likely feared that York wanted the crown, threatening her husband and son. Her chance to take control came in March 1456 when York's Protectorate ended. He wanted to pass a law taking back royal land granted to nobles and this lost him nobles' support. Nobles sympathising with Margaret took over leading positions in government and she moved the court away from London to the Midlands, where she had a lot of support.

However, neither Margaret nor York dared attack the other. If they did, they risked losing the sympathy and support of the 'middle-ground', the majority of the nobles who wanted peace. Even more importantly, whoever attacked might lose. The general desire for peace pressured York and Margaret into the 'Loveday' ceremony in March 1458. Compensation was agreed for the deaths at St Albans and the main figures walked to a service of forgiveness in St Paul's: York hand in hand with Margaret, Salisbury with the new young Duke of Somerset. One chronicler described the Loveday as 'a great comfort'. The 'comfort' didn't last.

In November Warwick was attacked in London, perhaps an assassination attempt by Margaret's supporters. He fled to Calais. Both sides spent the winter of 1458–9 preparing for war. When a Great Council was summoned to Coventry for June 1459, the Yorkists weren't invited and so feared they were to be charged with treason. War was about to begin.

Margaret's success: the battle of Blore Heath and the Coventry Parliament 1459

Fearing treason charges, the handful of Yorkist nobles gathered at York's castle in Ludlow. Salisbury, travelling from his lands in Yorkshire, was intercepted by a Lancastrian army but fought his way through at the battle of Blore Heath in September 1459. Warwick arrived with a contingent of professional soldiers from Calais, headed by the skilled, experienced Andrew Trollope. The Yorkist army then dug ditches and built barricades at Ludford Bridge on the edge of Ludlow, awaiting Margaret's army.

But there was no battle. When Trollope and the Calais garrison realised they were being asked to fight against King Henry (who was with the Lancastrian army) they marched away, leaving the Yorkists helpless. The Yorkist leaders ran. York headed for Ireland and Salisbury, Warwick and York's eldest son, 17-year-old Edward, Earl of March, took ship to Calais.

■ Annotate your graph to explain the pattern at November 1455, March 1456, March 1458, June 1459.

▽ **One major reason for the 'peace'**

Margaret

If I attack my enemies, many of the nobles may turn against me, giving my enemies the advantage.

York

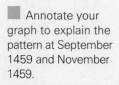

■ Annotate your graph to explain the pattern at September 1459 and November 1459.

In November 1459 Parliament met at Coventry and attainted the Yorkists. An Act of Attainder, passed by Parliament, was the most severe punishment possible. It convicted an individual of treason, which meant he would be executed if caught and all his lands were forfeit to the crown. His heirs could not inherit the land, so the whole family was impoverished for ever. This seemed a great success for Margaret, but had she made a mistake? Had she pushed the Yorkists into a corner, giving them no choice but to fight back and challenge Henry for the crown?

This Parliament was called the 'Parliament of Devils' in pro-Yorkist chronicles; no pro-Lancastrian chronicles exist to give a different view

Margaret

I have taken the crucial step against the Yorkist traitors.

Now we have been attainted, we have no choice but to fight – for the crown?

York

◁ **The situation after the 1459 Parliament**

York's bid for the throne: the battle of Northampton and the Act of Accord 1460

With their lives, lands and property at stake, the Yorkists had to fight back. Their supporters distributed propaganda sheets all over the south east, setting out how they'd been harshly treated but also proclaiming loyalty to Henry. In the spring of 1460, Salisbury, Warwick and young Edward of York landed in Kent and marched to London where they were greeted like heroes. They built up reinforcements and headed north. On 10 June 1460, the two armies met at Northampton in rain and mud. The Lancastrian guns became bogged down and ineffective, Lord Grey deserted to York and the battle turned into a rout. The Duke of Buckingham and other Lancastrian nobles were killed, including Lord Egremont. The Yorkists captured Henry and knelt before him, swearing loyalty, just as they had at St Albans. Henry was still king but now under Yorkist control. (Not everyone was fighting for king and honour: *Gregory's Chronicle* records that John Stafford loved Sir William Lucy's wife and took advantage of the battle to kill Sir William.)

York wasn't at Northampton. He'd stayed in Ireland. However, in October 1460, he returned and claimed the crown. After years of swearing loyalty to Henry, York now declared that he was the true king. He marched into Parliament, put his hand on the throne and turned to face the lords as if expecting applause, cheers and cries of 'Long Live King Richard'. Instead there was silence until the Archbishop of Canterbury asked York if he had come to see King Henry! York stormed out to take possession of the royal apartments.

The nobles met to decide on York's claim and finally reached a decision that shows how much they wanted to avoid any further warfare. They knew that choosing either Henry or York would lead to more conflict, so they chose both! The agreement, the Act of Accord, said that Henry would remain king for his lifetime but that York would be his heir. Henry's son, Prince Edward, was no longer Prince of Wales.

■ Annotate your graph to explain the pattern at June 1460, October 1460.

Egremont had caused much trouble in the north earlier in the 1450s; see page 48

For **York's claim**, see the royal family tree on page 38

York

I have won the right to be king. The Lancastrians were never the rightful kings.

I cannot accept the Accord. We must fight to keep the crown.

Margaret

△ The situation after the Act of Accord, autumn 1460

Annotate your graph to explain the pattern at December 1460, early February 1461, 17 February 1461.

Margaret's revenge: Wakefield and St Albans, December 1460–February 1461

The Accord never had a chance of preventing war. Margaret was certain to fight to protect her son's claim to the throne. Her support in the Midlands had reduced with the deaths at Northampton of Midlands noblemen like Buckingham but she raised troops in the north from the Earl of Northumberland, the northern rival of the Neville Earl of Salisbury. The young Duke of Somerset and others loyal to the Lancastrian family joined her. The fight was now for the crown.

The Lancastrians got their revenge at Wakefield on 30 December 1460. York had spent Christmas at his castle in Sandal near Wakefield but for some reason (perhaps to build up food supplies, perhaps he was tricked) he and his army were caught in the open by the Lancastrians. York and his second son, the 15-year-old Earl of Rutland, were killed. Salisbury was captured and executed. Their heads were stuck on spikes above Micklegate Bar in the city of York. Next, Margaret headed for London. En route her army pillaged towns and villages, driving off cattle and sheep for food. News of this devastation frightened Londoners into slamming the city gates shut.

The one Yorkist success came at the battle of Mortimer's Cross on the Welsh border, early in February 1461. A force of Lancastrians tried to block Edward, Earl of March from leading an army towards London. Edward was York's eldest son, tall, handsome and about to prove that he was a brilliant soldier. On the morning of the battle three suns were seen shining (see page 63 for explanation), a sight Edward immediately claimed as a sign of God's support and of victory to come. He was right. He won the battle and continued to London. (The handsome Earl of Wiltshire, who ran from St Albans in 1455, was even less brave at Mortimer's Cross, fleeing in disguise before the battle even started!)

By the time Edward arrived, Margaret had won the second battle of St Albans (17 February) and regained control of King Henry in what seems like a game of 'pass the parcel' with Henry as the parcel. However, deciding not to attack London, she and her army headed north, leaving London open to Edward.

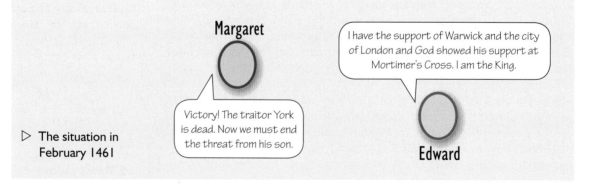

Margaret

I have the support of Warwick and the city of London and God showed his support at Mortimer's Cross. I am the King.

Victory! The traitor York is dead. Now we must end the threat from his son.

▷ The situation in February 1461

Edward

Edward IV and the Yorkist victory: Towton, March 1461

Before he reached London, Edward was joined by Warwick who had escaped from the battle of St Albans. They rode into London on 26 February and were 'joyously received'. Edward offered a fresh start, a young man who looked and behaved like a king, the complete opposite of Henry. They stayed in London just a few weeks, recruiting soldiers, summoning others to join them and proclaiming Edward as King Edward IV. The Yorkists said that the Lancastrians had forfeited the crown when they broke the Act of Accord by attacking the Duke of York at Wakefield.

Edward, Warwick and their army marched north. On Sunday 29 March the armies lined up on a wide plain of heathland at Towton, near Tadcaster in Yorkshire. The battlefield is open, windswept and chill on bright days but on that Palm Sunday snow howled in from the east, freezing fingers, blinding archers, obscuring visibility. The battle lasted all day, an unusually long time which tells us it wasn't an easy victory for Edward. We can't be certain why he won. It may have been the late arrival of the Duke of Norfolk's men, giving fresh impetus to the Yorkist army, but eventually the Lancastrians fled, many falling into the steep-sided valley of the River Cock where they were butchered by their pursuers. The heroic Andrew Trollope was among the dead. The handsome Earl of Wiltshire fled once more before the battle began but this time he was fatally slower! The Yorkists found him and cut off his head. When Margaret and Henry, who were in York, heard the news of defeat they fled to Scotland, leaving Edward in control of the battlefield and of England.

△ Whichever way a caltrop is dropped one spike sticks up, so they were scattered on battlefields to slow down charges by cavalry or foot-soldiers. *Gregory's Chronicle* contains one of the few detailed accounts of a battle and a caltrop in action. The author describes events and weaponry in detail and the heroism of Andrew Trollope who fought for Lancaster. According to the chronicle, Trollope was knighted for bravery but said, 'I do not deserve knighting. I only killed fifteen men because I trod on a caltrop and had to stand still in one place. That's why men had to come to me to fight but they're still here, lying dead all around me.'

■ Conclusions: What can we learn from the graph?

If you can't remember every detail immediately, don't worry. The graph on page 57 shows just how many twists and turns there were and it takes time to understand the pattern of events. Focus on understanding the general pattern and the critical turning points.

1 What evidence shows why each of these moments or decisions was important?
   a) Margaret's decision to call a Great Council at Coventry in June 1459
   b) York's decision to claim the crown in 1460
   c) Margaret's decision to turn north rather than risk attacking London.
2 What evidence shows why these statements are justified?
   a) The nobility wanted peace and would try any methods to avoid war.
   b) The Earl of Warwick played an important part in the Yorkists' success.
   c) The Yorkist success in 1461 was not inevitable.
3 Re-tell the story of 1455–61 in your own words to a set time limit. Creating a summary chart or visual aids may help focus on the essentials.

See pages 70–71 for what archaeology tells us about **Towton**

Edward became king because he won the battle of Towton. That's a very simple answer but true, because Edward's success was not guaranteed on the morning of Towton. However, he did have a chance, a good chance, and that's remarkable because only a month earlier the Yorkists seemed defeated: York himself was dead, Warwick had been beaten at St Albans, and the Lancastrians were dominant. So what gave Edward the chance of success at Towton and so led to his winning the crown?

The Activity on this page guides you through pages 62–69, helping you answer this question. This is a good task to do in collaboration with a friend or friends. You will find a concluding Activity on page 69.

1 Draw your own version of this chart, maybe on A3 paper.
2 As you read pages 62–69 note on your chart:
   a) how each factor contributed to Edward having a chance of success at Towton
   b) any links you can see between the factors
   c) how important you think each factor was.

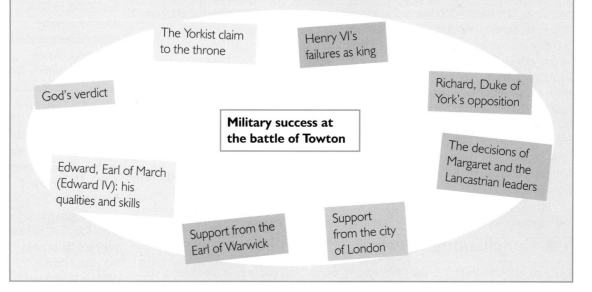

The Yorkist claim to the throne

Henry VI's failures as king

God's verdict

Richard, Duke of York's opposition

Military success at the battle of Towton

Edward, Earl of March (Edward IV): his qualities and skills

The decisions of Margaret and the Lancastrian leaders

Support from the Earl of Warwick

Support from the city of London

God's verdict and the Yorkist claim to the throne

Edward and his Yorkist supporters had no doubt why Edward was king. They said that God gave Edward victory because the Yorkists had the true and legitimate claim to the throne. The three suns shining at Mortimer's Cross had been the first sign that God favoured Edward. Victory at Towton was a second sign that God had declared for York and against Lancaster. Edward also said that he had a strong legal justification for being king. In November 1460 the Lords had sworn to uphold the Act of Accord, agreeing that York would inherit the throne after Henry's death. Edward said the Lancastrians had broken the Accord when they attacked York at Wakefield and so they had forfeited the crown. At Towton God had declared against these Lancastrian oath-breakers.

These arguments were helpful propaganda, valuable for influencing anyone undecided over whether to support Edward. We shouldn't underestimate their importance, even though they were used as propaganda or seem superstitious in today's world. Many Yorkists, marching to the battle or standing on the frozen ground at Towton, would

See page 38 for the **Yorkists' dynastic claim** to the throne

have taken encouragement from their belief in God's support. They believed they were in the right. However, it's also the case that the Yorkists had a practical reason for crowning Edward. Henry VI was no longer in their hands, as he'd been retaken by Margaret at St Albans, so the Yorkists couldn't say they were ruling on his behalf. They needed a king to avoid being called rebels, so they made their own!

■ How did belief in God's verdict help Edward's success?

Why did the Yorkist claim and the Act of Accord increase the Yorkists' chance of success?

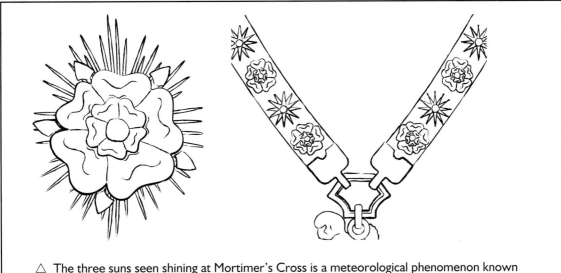

△ The three suns seen shining at Mortimer's Cross is a meteorological phenomenon known as parhelia. Edward's family already used the sun as one of their badges but after Mortimer's Cross Edward adopted the 'Sun in Splendour' as his main badge. It was worn by his supporters on their clothing or on livery collars, carved into wood and stone in buildings and displayed in stained glass windows (see the pictures on pages 5 and 76). Every 'Sun in Splendour' was a reminder of God's support for Edward and the House of York.

Henry VI's failure as king

Henry's failure is a vital part of the explanation for Edward's success because York and Edward would never have challenged Henry for the crown if he had been a successful king. However, Henry was not deposed simply because he was a failure. If that had been the case, he would have been deposed in 1450 (during Cade's rebellion) or in 1460 when York claimed the crown, the ideal opportunity for the nobility to get rid of Henry had they wished to do so. Simply being a bad king did not lead to deposition, so why was Henry's failure important?

The answer is that Henry's failures led to all the events and rivalries that came together at Towton to make Edward king. Henry's inability to lead allowed the rivalry between Somerset and York to escalate. His inability to stop feuds between his nobles led to York's gaining support from the Nevilles. These rivalries and feuds led to conflict in 1455 and ultimately the battles of 1459–61. Perhaps most importantly, Henry's inability to provide leadership led to Margaret's having to fill the vacuum as Lancastrian leader and ironically her decisions then played a vital part in her husband's deposition.

Richard of York's persistent opposition

The other important 'background' reason was Richard, Duke of York. To depose a king there needs to be an opposition and York created that opposition, eventually supported by the Neville earls, Salisbury and Warwick. At first York said that he wanted only to be one of the King's leading advisers but, in addition, he almost certainly also wanted to be seen as the King's heir and, after Prince Edward was born, the next-but-one in line for the throne.

It was this determination to be at the centre of government that seems to have alarmed Queen Margaret. Margaret seemingly feared that York wanted to take the crown from her husband and son and so, when they had the chance in 1459, her supporters in Parliament passed an Act of Attainder declaring the Yorkists traitors. Attainder meant loss of all lands and wealth and, in all likelihood, death. Thus, York had no real choice but to change the focus of his opposition. It was no longer a case of opposing other noblemen for the role of chief councillor but of opposing Henry, challenging his right to be king.

Henry's failings and York's opposition therefore created the possibility of the Yorkists taking the crown. But it is clear from the Act of Accord in November 1460 that the majority of the nobility wanted Henry to remain king. Some were so opposed that they fought to the death to defend him and they thought they had won when York was killed at Wakefield in December 1460. The Yorkist cause seemed over.

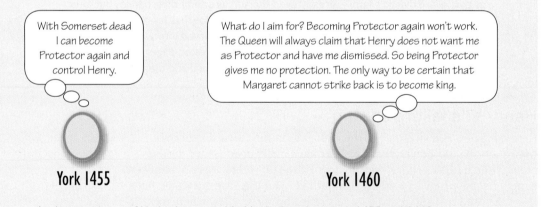

△ A comparison of likely changes in York's thinking between 1455 and 1460

How did Henry's failings and York's opposition help to create Edward's chance of success?

What links can you identify between the factors discussed so far? Add explanations of these links to your diagram (page 62).

Edward's qualities and skills

Why did York's son, Edward of March, succeed where York had failed? Three factors kept Edward in the fight and gave him a chance of deposing Henry: his own qualities and skills, the support of the Earl of Warwick and the support of the city of London.

Edward's first advantage was that he wasn't his father, Richard of York. York had spent ten years declaring his loyalty to Henry, only to make a dramatic about-turn in 1460, declaring that he was the rightful king after all. That made York look like a devious liar after all the times he'd denied accusations of treason, not an attractive prospect as king. In contrast, Edward wasn't tarnished by ten years of saying one thing before doing another. He was a fresh start and more! Aged 18, Edward was everyone's image of a king: tall, well-built, handsome and, on the evidence of Mortimer's Cross, an excellent soldier who had God's blessing. Even better, he was a man capable of taking decisions, the central task of a king and the one Henry had always failed to fulfil. An Italian visitor wrote two weeks after Towton: 'Words fail me to relate how well the common people love and adore him, as if he were their God.' Edward was a real, significantly better alternative to Henry and therefore an important factor in his own success. If York's son had been less kingly in appearance or a poorer soldier then his chances of success would have been much smaller.

Warwick's support

For all Edward's attractions, in 1461 people paid as much attention to his most powerful supporter, Richard Neville, Earl of Warwick. Warwick had played an increasingly prominent role since 1455, his importance shown by the possible Lancastrian attempt to assassinate him in 1458. He was by 1461 the most powerful, most influential nobleman in England, his lands and wealth enabling him to summon a very large number of fighting men. His control of Calais gave him both a refuge in time of difficulty (as after the Yorkists fled from Ludford in 1459) and the shipping to mount an invasion. Warwick also had a fame and charisma that no other nobleman possessed because of his raids on foreign ships in the English Channel.

Richard Neville, Earl of Warwick

He was extremely wealthy. After his father (Salisbury) was killed late in 1460, Warwick owned as much land as any other four earls. Whenever Warwick visited London he brought hundreds of men, all wearing his badge, the bear or bear and ragged staff, on their red jackets. In 1455 he was 27 years old, much younger than the other leading political figures who had spent decades working together to make up for King Henry's weaknesses. Perhaps therefore he was more ruthless, more likely to question the importance of remaining loyal to King Henry. Warwick also knew the importance of good propaganda. His attacks on foreign shipping in the Channel provided money to pay his men at Calais and won him great popularity in south-east England, where he was praised for defending England from attack.

In the mid-1450s, when the English yearned for leadership and military vigour, Warwick was the one leader who seemed capable of providing it, even if it was through what we would call piracy. Thus, Warwick's name and reputation were as important to Edward as the men and wealth he provided. His status is seen in newsletters from Milanese ambassadors, which declare that Warwick 'is like another Caesar in these parts' and that 'everything is in Warwick's power and he has done marvellous things'.

Warwick's support gave credibility to Edward's claim to the throne, not least in the eyes of many Londoners, but Warwick needed Edward at least as much as Edward needed him. Warwick was in a desperate situation, convicted of treason, close to losing everything. He had to fight on and, unable to become king himself, he needed someone who could. He needed Edward.

London's support for Edward

How did Edward, Warwick and London help to create Edward's chance of success?

What links can you see between the three factors?

What links can you see between these factors and those discussed earlier?

Why did Londoners slam the city gates against Margaret but open them to Edward? The immediate reason was fear of Margaret's northern army. Stories of the Lancastrian army looting property and destroying homes on its way south were bad enough but there were also rumours that Margaret's soldiers had permission to ransack London. However, the roots of London's hostility to Margaret and the Lancastrians went deeper. In 1456 she had moved the royal court to the Midlands, an insult to the capital and a considerable loss of trade to the city's businesses. Wealthy courtiers now spent their money in Coventry, not London. And there was a wider issue still: many London merchants believed that the Lancastrian government favoured foreign merchants over English ones. So Londoners believed they had strong economic reasons for opposing Lancaster, besides the fear of looting by Margaret's soldiers. They also had strong links with pro-Warwick merchants in Calais. Therefore London gave Edward men, money and credibility because he was proclaimed King Edward IV in the capital on 4 March 1461. No other town could have given Edward so much.

The decisions of Queen Margaret and the Lancastrian leaders

Between 1459 and 1461 Margaret and the Lancastrian leaders took a series of critical and difficult decisions. Two in particular, taken to strengthen the Lancastrian position, had consequences they didn't intend, putting Henry's hold on the throne at greater risk.

Acts of Attainder were Acts of Parliament that convicted individuals of treason. The attainted person was sentenced to death and his family could not inherit his lands and property

The first decision came in autumn 1459 when Margaret called a Great Council. She probably believed that the Lancastrians were now strong enough to end the Yorkist threat by convicting them of treason. When the Yorkists fled from Ludford, Margaret went ahead with Acts of Attainder at the Coventry Parliament. The treason charges must have seemed a good tactic, showing everyone the full treachery of the Yorkists and so increasing support for Henry and ending the Yorkist opposition.

But the Acts of Attainder rebounded on the Lancastrians because they forced the Yorkists to make a choice. Either they gave in, begging for mercy to get the charges overturned, or they fought back. And if they fought, they had to fight to win the crown. So, the treason charges unintentionally turned the conflict into a fight for the crown and so increased the chances of Henry's deposition. The Yorkists' attitude to the Coventry Parliament is shown by their calling it the 'Parliament of Devils'.

The attainders may also have had a second result that Margaret didn't anticipate: boosting support for her opponents. Until then, noble support for the Yorkists was very limited but the attainders may have played a part in persuading a small number of nobles (maybe six or eight at most) to move from being passive supporters of Henry to active supporters of York. Although we have no evidence of their thoughts and motives, they may have felt that the Yorkists had been harshly and unfairly treated by the Acts of Attainder. However, they would also have had more practical reasons for supporting York, notably the increasing evidence that the Yorkists had a chance of success. These half-dozen nobles fought for York in 1460–61, boosting the number of soldiers, and one of them, the Duke of Norfolk, may even have played a key part in the Yorkist victory at Towton.

The second key decision was the one that began this chapter. In February 1461 the Lancastrians decided to return north, leaving London open to Edward. It's easy to see this as the major mistake that handed Edward victory but at the time it must have seemed the better option. What were the arguments for and against attacking the capital?

The powerful argument in favour of attacking London was that success would give the Lancastrians control of the capital and stop Edward winning London's support and financial help. Controlling London would also boost confidence among Lancastrians and make them look successful. However, there were good reasons not to attack London:

- Could Margaret really order an attack on London? That could well increase support for the Yorkists and lead to prolonged warfare.

- The Lancastrians were very short of food. This was the middle of winter, so there was little food in the fields or hedgerows and few animals to catch. If they did not take London immediately, soldiers might desert to search for food. They might then be caught between London and Edward's approaching army.

- London and Margaret were hostile to each other: Margaret suspicious that London supported York, London resentful of Margaret's moving the court to the Midlands in 1456.

This was a difficult choice and the right answer was far from obvious, but so far the Lancastrians' decisions had been successful. They had killed York and beaten the famous Warwick. What else was there to fear? They could rebuild their strength in the north and be in an even stronger position to defeat Edward. Thus, they abandoned London to Edward but in doing so gave Edward a much stronger chance of success. Both these decisions were intended to crush the Yorkists but did a lot to help them. Even so, they did not guarantee Edward victory. Success or failure depended on events on the battlefield.

> If York had not been attainted would he have claimed the throne?
>
> Could Edward have won if Margaret had taken control of London?
>
> How did these decisions help to create Edward's chance of success?
>
> What links can you see between these decisions and any factors discussed earlier?

> For more detail on the **involvement of the nobles** in these battles see pages 70–71

The battle of Towton

Edward's success was not inevitable in March 1461. Despite all the reasons why Edward had a chance of becoming king – Henry's failings, York pushing the Yorkist claim, the support of Warwick and London, Margaret's decisions – a neutral observer would probably have said that he wasn't favourite to win. There were over twice as many nobles fighting for Henry as for Edward: 19 Lancastrians against 8 Yorkists.

In the end, it all came down to one day-long battle. Several factors played a part in Edward's victory. His own leadership, fighting from the front and inspiring his men, was important. The weather may have worked

▷ This modern illustration gives an idea of the sophistication of armour during the Wars of the Roses. As you can see, the armour had layers of over-lapping plates at the joints enabling the wearer to move easily. The best armour was tailor-made to fit an individual so that it gave maximum protection – a good incentive not to gain weight! As a result armoured knights were mobile, able to run and well-capable of getting up from the ground if knocked over. Almost all the fighting in the battles during the wars took place on foot because horses were too easy a target for archers. The only battle where a cavalry charge played an important part was Bosworth in 1485 (see pages 4–5 and 124–125).

The main problem with plate armour was that it made men vulnerable to heat, dehydration and exhaustion. Men could only fight for a short period before withdrawing from the front line for a rest and liquid. In one such moment at Towton, Lord Dacre was killed when he took off his helmet to have a drink and was hit by an arrow.

Armour of this kind also led to the development of the poll-axe, the weapon in this illustration. The poll-axe was a very flexible weapon as it had a sharp cutting edge on one side and a hammer-head on the reverse which could concuss an enemy even if he was wearing a helmet. The length of the shaft meant a poll-axe could be swung with enough momentum to kill even a soldier wearing full armour. In addition the end of the axe had a sharp point for stabbing through the joints in armour.

against the Lancastrians, as their archers were at a severe disadvantage, shooting into the wind and snow and probably uphill, unable to see in the snow where their arrows were landing and therefore shooting short. The late arrival of fresh Yorkist troops led by Norfolk may have galvanised the Yorkists at a critical moment. But we can't be certain why Edward won because we don't have detailed, reliable sources for the battle.

■ How important was Towton in Edward's winning the crown?

So, why did Edward win the crown?

Edward became king because he won the battle of Towton, but why was he in a position to win the battle? Several factors gave him that chance: the support of the city of London, of the Earl of Warwick and of a handful of other nobles. Their support was linked to Queen Margaret's decisions. But why was Margaret making decisions? It was because Henry was a total failure as king. Unfortunately for the Lancastrians, Margaret's decisions rebounded, strengthening the Yorkists instead of weakening them and giving them a chance of success. Finally, the military skills of the youthful, kingly Edward himself made the most of the chance on the battlefield. It all came down to one short March day on a snowy, bleak, frozen Yorkshire battlefield.

■ Concluding your enquiry

1 Look at your completed diagram. Which factor(s) had the most links to other factors?

2 Why did these factor(s) have the most links?

3 Where would you position each of the factors in the chart on page 62 on this table?

Factor/s that made Edward's success certain	
Factor/s that significantly contributed to Edward's success	
Factor/s that gave Edward a chance of success	
Factor/s that created the possibility of Henry being deposed	

4 Use the completed table to plan an answer to the Enquiry question, 'Why did Edward of York win the crown in 1461?'

The archaeology of Towton: how much do we really know about the battles?

Meet Towton 25. He spent his last day alive fighting amidst the snow at Towton, almost certainly in the Lancastrian army. He was 5' 9'' (175 cm) tall and aged between 36 and 45. This probably wasn't his first battle as he had a well-healed depression fracture on top of his head. At some stage during the battle he met a right-handed attacker and took five blows from a bladed weapon in face-to-face fighting. Finally, a large horizontal blade killed him with a blow to the back of his head, delivered with a slight down-to-up swing. Two more blows followed, one of which you can clearly see in the photograph, cutting deeply as it bisected his face, making sure he'd never breathe again.

This man was one of 37 skeletons discovered in 1996 when a garage was being built at a house on the edge of the battlefield at Towton. Archaeologists and other scientists have examined each skeleton minutely. The men's ages ranged widely, a third being under 25, a third aged 26–35 and a third 36–50. Their bones were more robust than most medieval skeletons, the result of regular strenuous exercise. Torn shoulder muscles and fractures typical of a javelin thrower suggest some were archers. Nine men also had well-healed skull injuries, including Skeleton 16 whose jaw had been sliced open by a sword earlier in his life, detaching his tongue and cutting through the roots of a large molar tooth. The wound had healed well, a tribute to the practical skills of medieval surgeons.

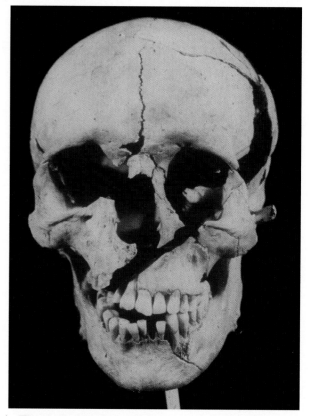

△ The skull of Skeleton 25, killed at Towton in 1461. Bodies had just been rolled into a mass grave. All were naked. No buckles, buttons or coins were found, just one silver finger ring.

How had these men died? Not from wounds to their torsos (defended by jacks – metal-lined jackets) but from blows to the head. Most had multiple wounds, probably suffered as they ran to escape at the end of the battle. Some blows were delivered after death, showing the savagery and fear of battle, although this is far from being peculiar to the Wars of the Roses.

Turning from the detail to the bigger picture, how many men fought at Towton that day in 1461? Towton is said to be the biggest battle ever fought in Britain but just how large was it? The sources don't help, giving numbers as high as 100,000 soldiers. This would have been perhaps 16 per cent of all adult men in the country, so whole villages would have been emptied if those numbers were true! Equally nonsensical are suggestions that 40,000 men died. This would have been twice the number killed by machine guns on the first day of the battle of the Somme in July 1916, a much longer day's fighting in summer sun compared to March gloom.

Andrew Boardman, in his book *The Battle of Towton*, suggests more reasonable figures: a total of 40,000 soldiers, with perhaps 10,000 dying in battle and another 5000 in the rout afterwards. Boardman rightly concludes, 'it is a very dangerous and fruitless enterprise for anyone to quote estimated figures on medieval battlefields with any accuracy and, in studying the battle of Towton, playing around with noughts only complicates the issue.'

Despite this uncertainty, it's clear that Towton was the largest battle of the period. Professor Colin Richmond compared the relative size of the battles of 1459–61 by counting the numbers of nobles involved. The table below sums up Professor Richmond's maths! It tells us that:

■ Blore Heath and Mortimer's Cross were much smaller battles

■ the numbers of nobles fighting in battles increased over time

■ Towton was the largest battle by some way despite the numbers being depleted by deaths, wounds and energies lost at the other battles fought since 1459.

Battle	Blore Heath 23/9/1459	Northampton 10/7/1460	Wakefield 30/12/1460	Mortimer's Cross 2 or 3/2/1461	St Albans 17/2/1461	Towton 29/3/1461
Total nobles	4	15	12	5	22	27
Allegiance	2L – 2Y	4L – 11Y	9L – 3Y	2L – 3Y	12L – 10Y	19L – 8Y

△ Key: L= Lancaster,
Y= Yorkist

The irony is that, thanks to archaeology, we know far more about the 37 individuals whose remains were excavated than we do about most of the 'bigger' questions about the battles: how large were the armies, what actually happened during the battle, why was this or that battle won and lost? The problem, as ever, lies in the sources. Accounts of battles are usually very brief, especially for the battles between 1459 and 1461. There are hardly any eye-witness accounts and even then it's impossible for an eye-witness to describe the reality or pattern of a battle. Add in the fact that open battlefields have few landmarks to aid description and you can understand why any good modern account of a battle is full of the words 'probably', 'possibly' and 'we can't be certain'.

Some books list Ludford Bridge (1459) as a battle but, as no fighting took place there, it hasn't been included in this table. However, the figures for the two sides are:

Ludford 12/10/1459 (no battle)
28
21L – 7Y

The view from 1461: looking backwards and forwards

Why was Henry VI so hard to depose?

Henry VI was an incompetent king for over 20 years yet many nobles still fought to keep him as king. This seems strange when other kings had been deposed (Edward II in 1327, Richard II in 1399). What was different about Henry? The answer lies in the actions of the kings. Other kings had pushed powerful opponents into corners, making them feel so threatened they had no choice but to fight back. But Henry VI was never going to push anyone into a corner and terrify them! So why was Henry deposed? Because, after 1459, the actions of Margaret and other Lancastrians made the Yorkists frightened for their lives and land (though, of course, they in turn had made Margaret frightened for the safety of her son and husband). This focus on mutual fear leads us back to our central question which was introduced on page 11: **if loyalty was so important and people did not want civil war, why did the Wars of the Roses take place at all?**

Now we've reached 1461 it's possible to suggest some answers so far.

1 A large part of the answer is fear, both in 1455 and 1459–61, fear of what others might do if they had power. The events of 1450 created mutual hostility and after that every action ratcheted up mutual fear. Fear drove York to strike first in 1455. Fear drove Margaret and the Lancastrians to take action in 1459, and then the need to survive drove the sequence of battles through to Towton.

2 Why was there fear? This takes us to the core of the explanation why fighting took place. It was because there was no effective king to create unity and stability, as this diagram shows:

Absence of effective king creating stability and unity

- Personal grievances flourished and could not be controlled
- Individuals with less sense of responsibility became 'loose cannons', capable of provoking violence
- Unexpected events caused anxiety and exaggerated problems
- Nobles wanted to be loyal to Henry but, if war broke out, did Henry look like a winner?

FEAR

3 Despite the battles, a great deal of thought and effort had gone into avoiding war. They tried negotiations and other ways of avoiding war but these all failed. Even so, when nobles did fight, many did so because it was their duty and because they were trying to solve the country's problems and restore order. Many had seen war in France and they weren't young men. Buckingham was 58, Salisbury 60 and York 49 when they were killed, so they weren't youngsters rushing naively into war. Their sense of duty is shown by the fact that 56 of the 70 nobles fought at least once (1 was too young, 7 too old, 2 mentally incapable, and the Earl of Worcester was in Italy buying books. More fought more often for Lancaster, suggesting a continuing strong loyalty to King Henry. Only 2 or 3 nobles changed sides, fighting for one side and then the other. This suggests that cynically choosing the likely winning side wasn't behind the choice of side.

4 In concentrating on why battles were fought and why Edward won (as required by examination awarding bodies), we've spent less time on questions about peace. For example, why did it take so long for the York–Somerset rivalry to lead to battle in 1455 and why did it take another four years after 1455 before another battle was fought? Understanding the absence of warfare is at least as important for understanding the people of the time and their ideas as studying why conflict began. This is why historians have recently spent much more time on exploring peace as well as war.

See pages 10–11 for a reminder of the **development of historians' ideas** on the period

Was fighting likely to continue after 1461?

The answer depended a great deal on the new king, young Edward IV, on his ability to provide leadership, fulfilling people's expectations of kingship and making effective use of the general desire to be loyal and to have peace. Could he:

Look back to pages 14–15 for a reminder of **what was expected of a king**

- **win the support of nobles previously loyal to Henry VI**, men like Thomas, Lord Roos who fought at Wakefield, St Albans and Towton, and who had been brought up with Henry and was probably motivated by a very personal loyalty

- **win the support of nobles whose relatives had been killed in battle**, men like the Duke of Somerset whose father had been killed at St Albans

- **put an end to feuds between nobles**, such as the Percy–Neville feud, that were creating instability and large-scale local violence

- **inspire confidence**, so that his decisions were respected and unexpected events did not lead to conflict

- **create a sense of continuity**, by producing male heirs so that disputes did not develop over who his heir would be?

Edward's task was far from easy. There had been ten years of uncertainty, anxiety and fear, all multiplied by the effects of the battles of 1459–61. Edward faced a very difficult task and, like every other king, would also face unexpected, unpredictable situations that he had no power over. His success therefore depended not just on his own choices but also on other's people's actions and decisions.

Where did the Roses come from?

The precise phrase 'The Wars of the Roses' doesn't seem to have been used before the 1800s but the idea goes back to the 1480s. All noblemen had badges (often several). The white rose was one of several Yorkist badges and Elizabeth of York used it as her personal badge. The red rose was particularly linked to the Beauforts and Henry VII's mother was a Beaufort. Therefore Henry and Elizabeth's marriage brought together the red and white roses. The earliest evidence of the idea of the warring roses comes from April 1486 when a Crowland Chronicle entry summed up Bosworth by saying, 'the tusks of the Boar were blunted and the red rose, the avenger of the white, shines upon us'. In the same month, Henry VII was greeted in the city of York by displays including two mechanical roses, the red rose (Henry) being made to spring up first before being joined by a white rose (Elizabeth of York). Who thought marketing and logos are modern inventions?

What happened next and who won the Wars of the Roses?

The problem with the term 'Wars of the Roses' is that it suggests there were always two sides, York and Lancaster, in constant conflict over who should be king. But, as you've discovered, the first battle in 1455 wasn't about who should be king at all. True, the battles of 1459–64 do fit the image of 'The Wars of the Roses' but after that the question of who fought who became a little more complicated!

The table gives you an outline of who fought who. Take your time to get a clear understanding of this as it will help you with Chapters 5–8. For 1469–71, focus on what was different about the sides and for 1483–87 on the question 'Who won in the end?' This seems an obvious and reasonable question to ask but there isn't a simple answer. We can't say York or Lancaster won because in 1485 (see below) there were Yorkists on both sides and Henry of Richmond (Henry Tudor) was as much the candidate of the house of York as of the house of Lancaster.

> ■ Some historians have suggested that the events of 1483–87 were not part of the Wars of the Roses, that they are a different conflict. Can you suggest why?

1455	LANCASTER and Beaufort **v.** YORK and Nevilles
	(Henry VI) (Somerset) (Richard of York) (Salisbury, Warwick)
St Albans	This phase of the conflict was not about the crown but about who would be Henry VI's chief councillor.

1459–64	LANCASTER and Beaufort **v.** YORK and Nevilles
	(Henry VI) (Somerset) (Richard, (Salisbury, Warwick) and the Tudors Edward of York)
Blore Heath Northampton Wakefield Mortimer's Cross St Albans Towton Hexham	This phase fits the name 'Wars of the Roses' most closely. It was a fight for the crown after Richard of York claimed the crown in 1460 but it was his son, Edward of York, who became Edward IV.

1469–71	LANCASTER, Beaufort and Nevilles **v.** YORK
	(Henry VI) (Somerset) (Warwick) (Edward IV) and the Tudors
Edgecote Barnet Tewkesbury	This conflict was created by Warwick's rebellion against Edward IV, leading to his alliance with the Lancastrians.

1483–87	LANCASTER, YORK, Beaufort, Tudor **v.** Ricardians and Nevilles
	(Henry, Earl of Richmond) (Richard III)
Bosworth Stoke	The Yorkists were split by Richard III's seizure of the crown. Therefore, many Yorkists allied with the remnants of Lancaster, Tudor and Beaufort against the supporters of Richard III who were mostly members of the former Neville affinity. So there were Yorkists on both sides!

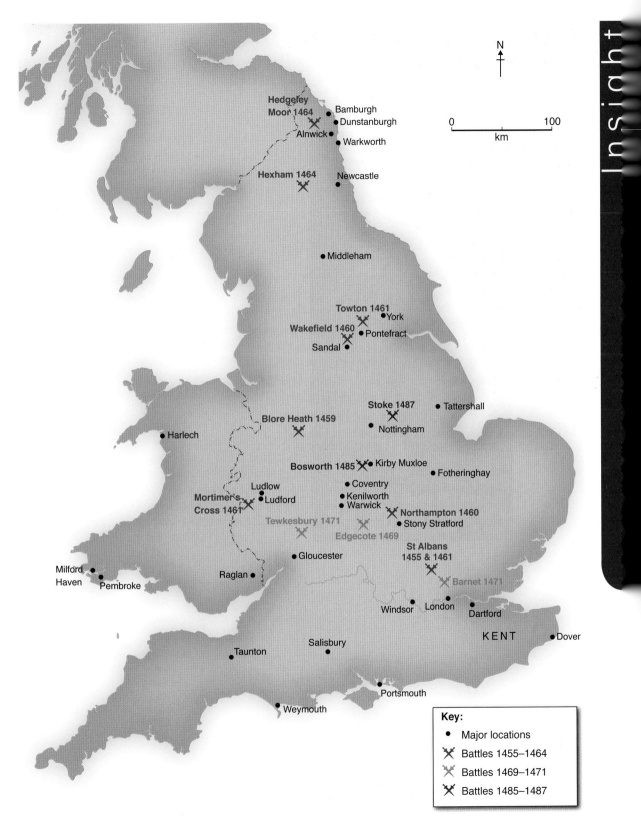

N

0   100
km

Hedgeley
Moor 1464
✘
Bamburgh
• Dunstanburgh
Alnwick •
• Warkworth

Hexham 1464
✘
• Newcastle

• Middleham

Towton 1461
✘ • York
Wakefield 1460
✘ • Pontefract
Sandal •

Stoke 1487
✘ • Tattershall
• Nottingham

Blore Heath 1459
✘
• Harlech

Bosworth 1485 ✘• Kirby Muxloe
• Fotheringhay

Ludlow •
• Coventry
Mortimer's • Ludford
• Kenilworth
Cross 1461 ✘
• Warwick
Northampton 1460
✘
Tewkesbury 1471 • Stony Stratford
✘
Edgecote 1469
✘
St Albans
1455 & 1461
✘
• Gloucester
Barnet 1471
✘
Milford
Haven •
Raglan •
Windsor • London •
Pembroke •
• Dartford

K E N T • Dover

Taunton •
Salisbury •

• Portsmouth

• Weymouth

Key:
•   Major locations
✘   Battles 1455–1464
✘   Battles 1469–1471
✘   Battles 1485–1487

5 Is Professor Carpenter right about Edward IV?

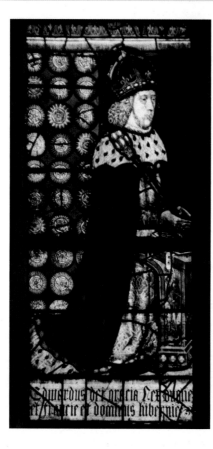

This stained-glass portrait of Edward IV from Canterbury Cathedral is both revealing and frustrating. Behind Edward we can see his badge – the sun in splendour – revealing how important this badge was to Edward. Frustratingly, however, the portrait does not show us Edward's true appearance. Like every other portrait it shows a flat, uninteresting face, very different from the reality.

What did Edward look like? He was 6' 3" (190 cm) tall, fair-haired, handsome, charming and elegant, probably the only English king with the looks and personality to play James Bond. Wherever he travelled, Edward left behind a trail of bewitched female admirers. Also like Bond, his quick-witted ruthlessness got him out of the tightest of corners. He'd fought his way to the crown in 1461, when the Yorkist cause seemed dead, and repeated this feat in 1471, as you'll read in chapter 6.

However, even this ideal candidate for kingship faced a huge task when, aged 18, he became king. Edward's task was to restore unity and order, and provide leadership and military inspiration, an awe-inspiring thought for other 18-year-olds! Edward had already proved himself an inspirational soldier but the events of the

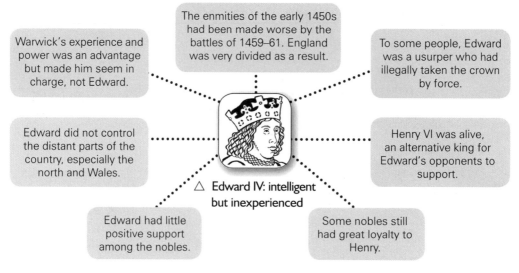

The enmities of the early 1450s had been made worse by the battles of 1459–61. England was very divided as a result.

Warwick's experience and power was an advantage but made him seem in charge, not Edward.

To some people, Edward was a usurper who had illegally taken the crown by force.

Edward did not control the distant parts of the country, especially the north and Wales.

Henry VI was alive, an alternative king for Edward's opponents to support.

△ Edward IV: intelligent but inexperienced

Edward had little positive support among the nobles.

Some nobles still had great loyalty to Henry.

1450s and especially the fighting of 1459–61 had created problems that would be very difficult even for this charismatic young man to overcome, as the diagram on page 76 shows.

Unsurprisingly Edward took over three years to end Lancastrian resistance. After he won the battle of Hexham in 1464, Margaret of Anjou and her son, Edward, fled to France. Henry VI was captured and imprisoned. However, success didn't last. In 1469 the Earl of Warwick rebelled. His attempt to control Edward failed, but Edward did not punish Warwick.

Then Warwick fled to France where he made an extraordinary alliance with his old enemy, Margaret of Anjou. In 1470 Warwick invaded England with French help, forcing Edward to flee to Burgundy. Henry VI was made king again. Edward was a near-penniless exile.

All this reads as if Edward's reign had been a disaster, the task too much for an inexperienced youngster. Yet here's the verdict of one eminent historian, Professor Christine Carpenter of the University of Cambridge:

Edward did not lose his throne in 1470–71 because he had misgoverned in his first period as king. Inheriting an extremely difficult situation, he had dealt with it with remarkable aplomb, especially for one so young and inexperienced. He had coped expertly with both Lancastrian resistance and the foreign interference which exploited this and secured the northern border. Good management had made his finances perfectly adequate for his needs and the resistance to his rather high-handed use of taxation had only become a serious matter towards the end of the decade because of the participation of other much more dangerous forces. Far from throwing away all the confiscated lands at his disposal on his accession, he had used them astutely to build up a Yorkist nobility, while wisely realising that he had to turn the whole nobility into his men and needed therefore to forgive and restore some of his former enemies or their heirs. The defection of pardoned Lancastrians was simply the price that had to be paid for the only possible policy, as long as there was a rival for them to defect to. Neither Warwick nor the Woodvilles had been allowed to dominate him, and his closest associates in governance had increasingly become his new nobles, Hastings above all. Given the circumstances, he had done well with the problem of restoring order, but that was something that could only be properly tackled once he was in a more secure position with regard to the nobility. There had been the odd error and misjudgement, such as failing to kill Henry VI as soon as he had him in his custody and perhaps being a little casual about the extent of rebellion in 1469 and 1470, but surprisingly few considering his age and lack of experience.

◁ Christine Carpenter, *The Wars of the Roses* (1997), pages 180–81

1 The use of red picks out positive comments, blue identifies negative comments, words underlined describe Edward's skills. What do the underlinings and the balance of colour tell you about Professor Carpenter's verdict on Edward?

2 How would you sum up Professor Carpenter's view on Edward's kingship?

■ **Enquiry Focus:** Is Professor Carpenter right about Edward IV?

Professor Carpenter's verdict that Edward was a success seems puzzling. How could Edward have been a success and yet still be deposed in 1470? Surely a success would have kept his crown, not fled for his life? This enquiry examines the key aspects of Edward's reign to test Professor Carpenter's verdict. Making detailed notes will be essential but using the Success/Failure line below is just as important, helping you see the 'big picture' of the arguments and reach an overall conclusion, and stopping you getting lost in the details. (Note the seven aspects are not positioned on the line.)

1 Draw the Success/Failure line. Re-read Professor Carpenter's summary and decide where on the line she would put the aspects of Edward's reign, as shown in the boxes. (Note that two, Marriage and Splendour, are not discussed in the extract on page 77, so leave them out here. They are all discussed in this enquiry.)
2 Read pages 79–89. Place each of the seven aspects of Edward's reign where you think they go on the line. Make notes to justify your choices and list anything that makes the placement choice difficult.
   You will find a concluding Activity on page 89.

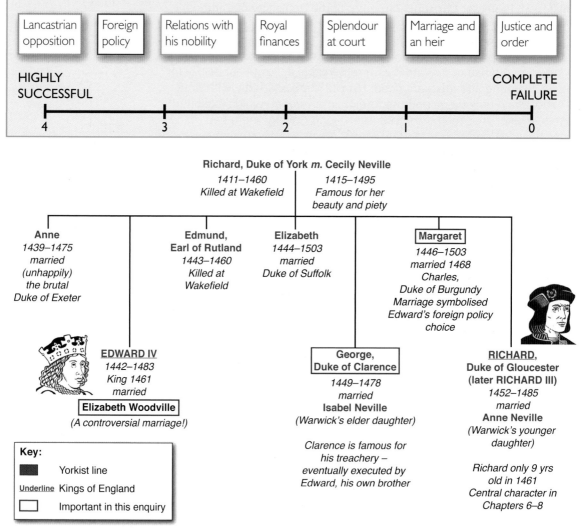

| Lancastrian opposition | Foreign policy | Relations with his nobility | Royal finances | Splendour at court | Marriage and an heir | Justice and order |

HIGHLY SUCCESSFUL   **COMPLETE FAILURE**

4   3   2   1   0

Richard, Duke of York *m.* **Cecily Neville**
1411–1460
Killed at Wakefield
1415–1495
Famous for her beauty and piety

Anne
1439–1475
married (unhappily) the brutal Duke of Exeter

Edmund, Earl of Rutland
1443–1460
Killed at Wakefield

Elizabeth
1444–1503
married Duke of Suffolk

Margaret
1446–1503
married 1468 Charles, Duke of Burgundy Marriage symbolised Edward's foreign policy choice

EDWARD IV
1442–1483
King 1461
married
Elizabeth Woodville
(A controversial marriage!)

George, Duke of Clarence
1449–1478
married
Isabel Neville
(Warwick's elder daughter)

Clarence is famous for his treachery – eventually executed by Edward, his own brother

RICHARD, Duke of Gloucester
(later RICHARD III)
1452–1485
married
Anne Neville
(Warwick's younger daughter)

Richard only 9 yrs old in 1461 Central character in Chapters 6–8

Key:
■ Yorkist line
<u>Underline</u> Kings of England
☐ Important in this enquiry

△ Edward IV's parents, brothers and sisters. Although he was the first Yorkist king, Edward did not present himself as the head of a new dynasty, a new royal line. Instead he emphasised continuity, but the continuity was from Richard II, not Henry VI. Genealogical charts portray Edward as a return to the 'proper' royal line, interrupted when Henry IV (the first Lancastrian king) usurped the crown by deposing Richard II (see family tree on page 38).

Lancastrian opposition: how successful were Edward's tactics?

Despite his victory at Towton Edward still faced considerable opposition. The Lancastrian royal family provided a focus for resistance to Edward, especially as they expected aid from Scotland and France, the latter because Margaret was a member of the French royal family. Major figures such as the Duke of Somerset continued to support Henry, encouraged by Henry and Margaret's escape to Scotland.

Edward therefore had to work hard to overcome opposition. In 1462 Edward ordered the execution of the Earl of Oxford and his son after new Lancastrian plots were discovered. Then Edward marched his army north when a Lancastrian–Scottish force invaded England, capturing the formidable castles at Alnwick, Dunstanburgh and Bamburgh. Although Edward caught measles and handed over the leadership to the Nevilles (Warwick and his younger brother John), the invaders were stopped and the castles recaptured. Finally, William Herbert, one of Edward's strongest supporters, defeated opposition in Wales, though even there Harlech Castle in north-west Wales held out for Lancaster.

Despite the Lancastrian plots, Edward was generous to Lancastrian nobles whenever possible, aiming to win them over to his side. He made a particular effort with two men. One was Henry Beaufort, Duke of Somerset. If Edward won Somerset's loyalty it would be a huge blow to other Lancastrians. The other was Sir Ralph Percy, head of the Percy family while the Earl of Northumberland was a child. Percy loyalty was crucial as a defence against Lancastrian invasion in the north east.

Somerset was welcomed at court, joining Edward in hunting and jousting and sharing the same sleeping quarters. Percy was given back Bamburgh and Dunstanburgh Castles as a sign of Edward's willingness to trust him. It didn't work. Somerset fled back to Henry. Percy handed over his castles to the Scots. So a military solution was needed in the north. Lancastrian resistance was finally defeated by Montagu at the battles of Hedgeley Moor and Hexham in 1464. Somerset, Percy and other Lancastrians were executed. Margaret and Prince Edward fled to France. Henry, after a year in hiding, was captured in July 1465 and imprisoned.

However, support for Lancaster hadn't ended. In 1468 Louis XI of France seemed about to give aid to Margaret. This encouraged more Lancastrian plots against Edward, one involving Lord Wenlock (a supporter of Warwick), another the Hungerford and Courtenay families and the new Earl of Oxford, all Lancastrian loyalists, and yet another apparently swirling round a London alderman, Thomas Cook. There was also increased disorder in a number of counties (see page 82). This all suggested the threat would continue as long as Henry and Prince Edward were alive.

Edward had shown determination and flexibility in dealing with Lancastrian opposition yet he hadn't put an end to it. To a large extent this was for reasons related to past events that were outside his control:

- Continuing loyalty to Henry. Some nobles and gentry saw Edward as a **usurper**. This undermined his authority and made people doubt whether he could last on the throne.

- Past enmities and deaths in the battles of 1455–61 meant that some nobles believed they could never be accepted as loyal to Edward, so for them opposition felt the only option.

See map on page 75 for **battles and castles**

John Neville was Warwick's capable younger brother; he was ennobled as Lord Montagu in 1461

Somerset was the son of the duke killed at St Albans in 1455

The young **Earl of Northumberland's** father was killed at Towton and his grandfather at St Albans in 1455

usurper
Someone who seizes the crown illegally

conciliation

Winning over, in this case to support Edward

When kings were deposed

Previous deposed kings, e.g. Richard II, had 'disappeared' but this didn't stop rumours that they were alive, leading to opposition rebellions. And Richard had been unpopular, but Henry himself wasn't

■ Place 'Lancastrian opposition' on your Success/Failure line. Think about the difficulty of the task before deciding. Also consider whether the placing of the topic would differ in 1465 and 1468. Make notes to support your choice of position.

This suggests that ending opposition was a very difficult task. Even so, some historians have criticised Edward but, for each criticism (in bold) below, there are also strong arguments in favour of his actions:

■ **Over-confidence in his ability** to win over his enemies. However, **conciliation** had clear advantages. It was faster and cheaper than fighting and met public expectations that Edward would restore unity, not increase divisions.

■ **Relying on the Nevilles too much** and not doing enough himself militarily, so increasing the perception that Warwick was at least as important as Edward. However, Edward could not be everywhere and the Nevilles were successful.

■ **His failure to execute Henry**. Professor Carpenter suggests that execution would have ended opposition but was executing 'Harmless Henry' a political possibility? True, there had been executions aplenty after battles but no executions of innocents in cold blood – and Henry was seen as an innocent. Edward may have feared that executing Henry would outrage nobles and gentry and increase support for Prince Edward of Lancaster, aged 12 in 1465 and nearing adulthood.

Marriage: a major mistake?

Most English kings married foreign princesses to create alliances and increase diplomatic influence. Discussions were taking place for a marriage between King Edward and Bona of Savoy, sister of Louis XI of France, when news broke in September 1464 that Edward had married Elizabeth Grey in secret. It was said that Edward married her because she refused to join the long list of his mistresses. Lust, maybe love, had seemingly decided whom Edward married, not diplomacy.

Elizabeth is usually known as **Elizabeth Woodville**, her maiden name, though in 1464 she was Elizabeth Grey, the widow of Sir John Grey

△ Elizabeth Woodville (c.1437–92) was about 27 when she married the 22-year-old king. Her family proved a problem for Edward because it was easy for opponents to criticise them. This was summed up by the story of a jester at court who walked in wearing very high boots. He explained that he had to wear them because the 'Rivers were so high'. Rivers was the title of Elizabeth's father; the message in the 'joke' being that the Woodvilles had far too much influence.

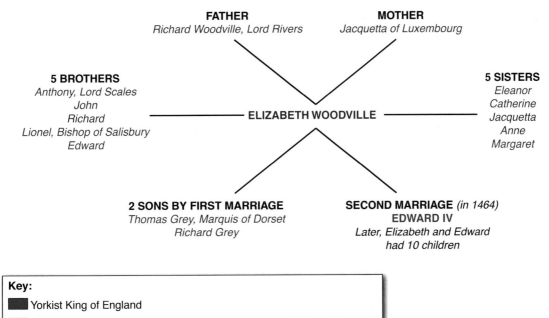

FATHER
Richard Woodville, Lord Rivers

MOTHER
Jacquetta of Luxembourg

5 BROTHERS
Anthony, Lord Scales
John
Richard
Lionel, Bishop of Salisbury
Edward

ELIZABETH WOODVILLE

5 SISTERS
Eleanor
Catherine
Jacquetta
Anne
Margaret

2 SONS BY FIRST MARRIAGE
Thomas Grey, Marquis of Dorset
Richard Grey

SECOND MARRIAGE *(in 1464)*
EDWARD IV
Later, Elizabeth and Edward
had 10 children

Key:
■ Yorkist King of England
■ Elizabeth Woodville's relatives living when she married Edward in 1464
Edward IV had to decide how to reward all these relatives

△ This diagram shows the numbers of the Queen's relatives in 1464. (When I taught students about the Woodvilles I used teddy bears to help them remember the scale of the Woodville family. One student who acted as Elizabeth Woodville had to catch a series of soft toys I threw in her direction – two for her sons, one for her father, etc. As she disappeared behind a mountain of soft toys it became very clear just how large the Woodville family was.)

The practical problem facing Edward was how to reward Elizabeth's family at a level suitable for royal relatives but not so great that it created resentment among noble families. For the most part Edward succeeded. Elizabeth herself was not extravagant, keeping a modest household and mostly playing the conventional queenly role, in the background of politics. Edward did promote the Queen's father, Lord Rivers, to the rank of Earl and made him both Constable and Treasurer of England. Her brother, Anthony, a renowned jouster, cultured and highly educated, took a leading role at court but overall the Woodvilles were not showered in grants of lands and offices.

The Woodvilles did gain from marriages because nobles wanted the kudos of marrying into the royal family. Elizabeth's sisters married into noble families, raising the Woodvilles' status and making Edward useful alliances with noble families without costing him a penny. Warwick, however, may not have been so pleased. He may have hoped to marry one of his daughters to the wealthy Duke of Buckingham but lost out to a Woodville girl. He intended his nephew (Montagu's son) to marry the wealthy Holland family heiress but she was scooped up by Thomas Grey, the Queen's elder son. Finally, Warwick's 65-year-old aunt, the widowed Duchess of Norfolk, was married off to 18-year-old John Woodville. This must have looked as if Warwick couldn't even protect his aunt from exploitation.

Yes, you're allowed to be confused by the **many Woodvilles**! Read this slowly and don't panic!

The Woodville marriage was not a financial error for Edward but it was a problem in other ways:

- He had failed to use his marriage to gain diplomatic advantages.

- It appeared an 'unkingly' marriage. In 1461 there'd been hope Edward would provide stability, good decision-making, real leadership. Instead this furtive marriage suggested weakness, lack of judgment and, through its secrecy, a lack of confidence, perhaps even that Edward was afraid of Warwick.

- It gave Warwick a great propaganda advantage in 1469–70 when he rebelled. It was easy for his propaganda to portray the Woodvilles as greedily dominating a weak Edward and therefore excluding the old noble families from power.

Ironically, given that Elizabeth had two sons by her first marriage, one benefit Edward didn't gain from his marriage was a male heir early in his reign. Although Edward couldn't be accused of not trying, perhaps the lack of a prince made Edward seem more vulnerable when Warwick was considering rebellion.

■ Place 'Marriage and an heir' on your Success/Failure line. Think about whether people's perceptions of the Woodvilles were more important than the marriage itself. Make notes to support your choice of position.

Justice and order

The system of law, justice and punishment was dependent on the king for leadership. His energy and efforts determined how successful it was. Edward took his responsibility to the law seriously, promptly visiting troublesome areas early in his reign, showing determination to put an end to disorder and crime. Early in the reign, when John Paston twice ignored Edward's command to explain his role in a dispute, Edward exploded, 'If you come not at the third commandment you shall die.' Paston rapidly arrived at court. Such strength was vital for building confidence in his kingship and showing that he was providing better government than Henry VI. However, by the end of 1467, disorder and lawlessness was increasing in many regions. A violent feud between Lord Grey of Codnor and the Vernon family in Derbyshire spread to nearby counties and seemed out of control. Percy **retainers** caused trouble in Yorkshire when they refused to pay rents. The commons of Kent rioted against Earl Rivers (the Queen's father) in 1468 for his 'heavy lordship', his harsh treatment of his tenants. Similar complaints were made against other courtier lords, echoing the grievances of Cade's rebels in 1450 against Henry VI's courtiers.

In response Edward did the right things. He set up commissions to investigate and punish law-breakers, made a law to reduce retaining, and used bonds to force landowners to obey the law (they promised to pay a bond, a large fine, if they broke the law and thus were 'encouraged' to keep the peace). But disorder continued. Did this reduce confidence in Edward or was it a sign that confidence was falling? Whichever it was, disorder suggested that Edward was failing to live up to the high expectations of 1461.

retainers
Members of a lord's affinity who wore his badge. All lords needed retainers but they could be used as soldiers in private feuds. See page 13

Royal finances

Today finance is a critical part of government but it was less important to a medieval king. Provided he had enough money to pay for his household and could persuade Parliament to raise taxes in wartime, there were no financial crises. There was a good deal about Edward's financial policies that was successful, despite the economic recession that affected trade and agriculture, the main components of the economy. The result of this recession was that Edward had less income. That from customs revenues (an important part of his income) fell because there was less trade, partly because of a trade war with Burgundy which was eventually settled when Edward made an alliance with Burgundy. Edward's policies went some way to making up for this deficit: he reduced the costs of his household (which had fewer 'hangers-on' than in Henry VI's day) and developed a more efficient administration of the royal lands to maximise income. Such improvements were useful and worthwhile but unremarkable. They certainly didn't determine his success or failure as king.

Public awareness of royal finances was greatest when the king asked Parliament for taxation for defence or for an attacking war. This meant tax was collected from everyone and, because this might happen only once every three or four years, people were much more aware of paying tax and what it was spent on. Parliament granted Edward two taxes, in 1463 for war against Scotland and in 1468 for war against France. Neither war took place because rebellions meant that Edward had to focus on dealing with Lancastrian opposition. Instead, the money went into Edward's pocket to contribute to his household expenses. This was not his intention when asking for the taxes but this is what happened and it undoubtedly caused complaint and dissatisfaction, adding to the sense that Edward was not in control and not behaving as a good king should.

Splendour at court

A king was expected to look as rich as possible, displaying his wealth openly as a sign of England's strength. Edward had natural advantages in his height and good looks, enabling him to show off richly embroidered, colourful clothes in the latest fashions. He fully realised the importance of spectacle and his court in the 1460s was a great centre of display and wealth although it was to reach even greater heights in the 1470s. Lavish tournaments (with jousting the centrepiece) were particularly important for showing that Edward was a match for any ruler in Europe. One particularly grand tournament was held as part of Edward's attempts to win over the Duke of Somerset in 1463. Others marked Queen Elizabeth's coronation in 1465 and the arrival of Burgundian ambassadors in 1467 when England's leading jousters, including Thomas Stanley and Anthony Woodville (the Queen's brother), took on Burgundy's men.

> ◼ Place 'Justice and order', 'Royal finances' and 'Splendour at court' on your Success/Failure line. Think about whether the placing of any of the topics would differ in 1465 and 1468. Make notes to support your choice of positions.

Foreign policy

Foreign policy options

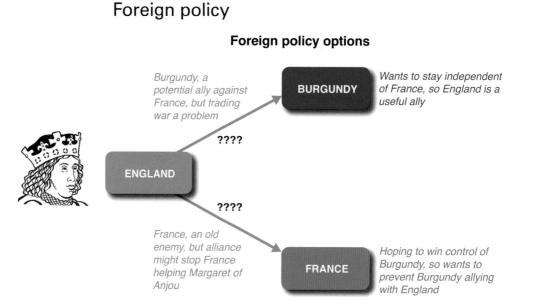

Burgundy, a potential ally against France, but trading war a problem

BURGUNDY — *Wants to stay independent of France, so England is a useful ally*

????

ENGLAND

????

France, an old enemy, but alliance might stop France helping Margaret of Anjou

FRANCE — *Hoping to win control of Burgundy, so wants to prevent Burgundy allying with England*

The main decision facing Edward was whether to ally with France or with Burgundy, an independent duchy fighting to stay independent from France. Tradition suggested enmity towards France and therefore alliance with Burgundy but there were major trading problems between England and Burgundy, with English cloth banned from being sold in Burgundy. Through the mid-1460s Edward negotiated with both potential allies, playing them against each other to get the best terms. Warwick acted as his chief negotiator with France, Earl Rivers (the Queen's father) with Burgundy. It wasn't until 1467 that Edward made his decision. While Warwick continued negotiations with King Louis of France, a Burgundian delegation arrived in London and was greeted with great ceremony. Soon afterwards Edward agreed the first stage of a treaty with Burgundy. This included the marriage of Edward's sister, Margaret, to Duke Charles of Burgundy and the end of the trade war, bringing benefits to English merchants.

This foreign policy decision marks the beginning of the serious split between Edward and Warwick. Edward dismissed Warwick's youngest brother, George Neville, Archbishop of York, from his post as Chancellor and Warwick himself left court in July 1467, not returning until early 1468. On top of Warwick's problems in finding husbands for his daughters (see page 81), the Burgundian alliance was a public demonstration that he did not have as much influence with Edward as he (and most others) had assumed. It was soon after this that rumours began circulating in France that Warwick was contemplating an alliance with Margaret of Anjou to put Henry VI back on the throne.

Such an alliance seems unlikely early in 1468. It's just as likely that this was a piece of French mischief designed to cause trouble in England at a time when it seemed that Edward was seriously contemplating war with France. At the same time, King Louis sent help to Lancastrians in Wales, another way of distracting Edward.

■ Place 'Foreign policy' on your Success/Failure line. How might the placement differ from 1468 to 1470 when France had played a part in Edward's deposition? Make notes to support your choice of position.

Overall, Edward had handled foreign policy issues well but they demonstrate that Edward could not control everything. He may have taken the best decisions on behalf of England but this did not stop Warwick from disagreeing with the decision or this disagreement from feeding into other grievances that led him eventually to rebellion.

Edward's relationship with his nobility

Effective government depended on the quality of the bond between king and nobles. This relationship worked best when the nobles had high respect for the king and when he listened to their advice and used them to ensure justice and order in their localities and as his leaders in wartime. Building this relationship was vital for Edward but far from easy. Some leading nobles were still Lancastrian, others (Buckingham, Northumberland, Norfolk) were young children, making Edward look over-dependent on one noble family, the Nevilles. Edward therefore needed to build up a wider body of supportive nobility, men who controlled every region of the country on his behalf.

Edward IV's family	Woodvilles: relatives by marriage	Nevilles	New nobles: created by Edward	Older noble families
Edward's brothers: George, Duke of Clarence (20 in 1469) Richard, Duke of Gloucester (17 in 1469) Uncles by marriage: Henry Bouchier, Earl of Essex Thomas, Archbishop of Canterbury	Earl Rivers Anthony, Lord Scales	Richard, Earl of Warwick His brothers: John, Lord Montagu George, Archbishop of York Warwick's uncle: William, Lord Fauconberg	William, Lord Hastings William, Lord Herbert Humphrey, Lord Stafford Walter, Lord Ferrers John, Lord Dinham John, Lord Wenlock Walter, Lord Mountjoy	Over 50 nobles (the majority): Some still supported Henry after 1461, e.g: Somerset Exeter Clifford Roos Nobles who were still children: Buckingham Norfolk Northumberland

The most important figures amongst the new nobles Edward created were William, Lord Hastings and William, Lord Herbert (made Earl of Pembroke in 1468). Hastings, the King's closest friend and adviser, was head of Edward's household and acquired widespread lands and power in the Midlands. Herbert controlled Wales for Edward, a crucial role in a potentially rebellious region.

Edward's attitude to Lancastrians was generous too, sensibly aiming to win over individuals rather than push them into permanent enmity. Former opponents, such as Lords Rivers and Stanley, were welcomed to court and the family of the executed Earl of Oxford was allowed to keep their family lands. Edward was also cautious in the rewards he gave to the new Woodville nobles, who received little power by way of land and posts.

George, Duke of Clarence is usually known by his title, Clarence

In contrast, he lavished land on his brother, George, Duke of Clarence (aged 15 in 1464), who was soon expected to play a major role in his brother's government. The third brother, Richard (born 1452), received titles but was too young to be given authority.

All this seems straightforward but the reality of handling individuals was complex. The example of Warwick's brother, John, shows how difficult Edward's decisions were. In 1461 John was made Lord Montagu. Then, in 1464, after he beat the Lancastrians at the battle of Hexham, he was made Earl of Northumberland. This was the title held for generations by the Percy family and John was also given much of their land in the north east. It seemed that Edward had won John's loyalty because, when Warwick rebelled in 1469 and early in 1470, John refused to join his brother. However, after the second rising, Edward decided to give back the title of Earl of Northumberland to the Percy heir since the Percy family (because of its long-standing links to local gentry) was most likely to ensure that the north east stayed loyal to Edward. Logical though it was, Edward's decision was a blow for John Neville. Edward gave John alternative rewards – the grand title of Marquis Montagu and lands in Devon and the south west – but to John it seemed, according to one chronicler, a 'magpie's nest', all flash and glitter on the surface but of no real value. When Warwick rebelled for the third time, John turned against Edward and allied with his brother. So what had seemed a good decision to bring back Percy rebounded on Edward.

A more general criticism of Edward's handling of his nobility is that for all his efforts he did not build up enough committed support amongst the nobles. Too many stood by and watched in 1470 when Warwick chased him from the throne. We have seen how nobles were prepared to die for Henry VI but far fewer put their lives on the line for Edward. True, he'd been king for only nine years but perhaps by then he'd been less convincing as king than Professor Carpenter suggests, leading to his nobles doubting his chances of dealing with Warwick.

■ Place 'Relations with his nobility' on your Success/Failure line. Before you decide, think about how difficult Edward's task was, given Lancastrian opposition. Make notes to support your choice of position.

Edward and Warwick: why did Warwick rebel?

To understand the events of Warwick's rebellions it helps to think of three phases:

1. 1469 – Warwick rebelled, along with Edward's own brother, George, Duke of Clarence. They defeated Edward's army at Edgecote (July 1469) and executed its commanders. Edward wasn't there but was captured afterwards. Warwick tried to rule with Edward as his prisoner but lawlessness increased and his government was ignored, so he had to free Edward.

2. 1470 – Warwick tried again, taking advantage of a rebellion in Lincolnshire. This time he probably intended to make Clarence king but failed. He fled to France, where he made an extraordinary alliance with his old enemy, Margaret of Anjou, aiming to restore Henry VI to the throne.

3. 1470 – Warwick invaded England with French help, forcing Edward to flee to Burgundy. Henry VI was king again.

Initially Edward had rewarded Warwick lavishly with important posts such as Great Chamberlain and Admiral of England. Warwick remained Captain of Calais, received widespread lands and was at the centre of Edward's government but their relationship worsened as a result of decisions by the

King. Each or all of these may have led Warwick to rebel, though we have to be cautious in making judgments as we have no evidence for Warwick's exact motives:

- Warwick's plans for family marriages were ended by Woodville marriages (see page 81).

- In 1467 Edward dismissed Warwick's brother, George, from his post as Chancellor, a sign of Edward's wanting to be seen as independent of the Nevilles.

- Warwick had no sons but hoped that his elder daughter, Isobel, would marry Edward's brother, Clarence. Edward turned down the idea, wanting Clarence to marry a foreign princess. This, from a national viewpoint, was a good decision of Edward's but it showed little awareness of Warwick's need to build his family's future.

- Hastings, Herbert, Stafford and Rivers all gained influence with the King, seemingly reducing Warwick's influence. Warwick's execution of Herbert, Stafford, Rivers and Sir John Woodville in 1469 suggests he bitterly resented their rise but he probably had simpler motives: to eliminate some of Edward's most reliable supporters.

- Edward's decision to ally with Burgundy (see page 84) rather than with Warwick's choice of France.

A second question we need to ask is why Warwick thought he could rebel and win. He must have been confident to put his life, lands and power at stake, everything his family had built up through generations. So why did he think he would succeed? What does this tell us about how Edward's kingship appeared in 1469?

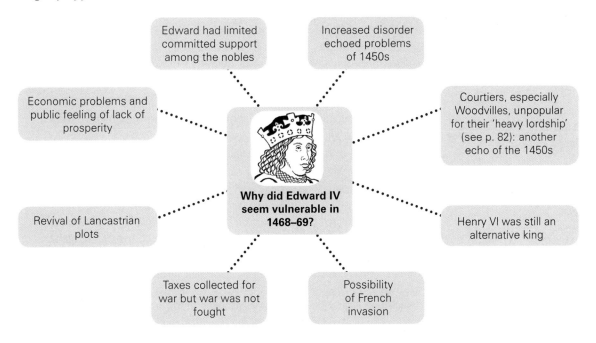

△ It looked as if Edward had not overcome the problems he faced when he became king

The chart on page 87 suggests why Warwick may have seen Edward as weaker in 1468 than when he became king in 1461 and why Warwick may have feared that Edward would be in real danger if there was a Lancastrian rebellion or a French invasion. If Edward lost then Warwick too would lose all he'd gained. Therefore, his first rebellion in 1469 probably resulted from not mere ambition but a need for self-defence and perhaps a wish to create a stronger regime that would make a better fist of government.

Warwick's first rebellion in 1469 failed but it was still a giant leap from there to alliance with his old enemy Margaret. The reason for making this leap may lie in the events in between. Edward had not punished Warwick immediately but Warwick must have been anxious. He couldn't be sure Edward would remain so forgiving. Then came Warwick's involvement in the Lincolnshire rebellion in 1470. As he'd been rebellious twice over, he could no longer stay in England. Where could he go and what could he do? We often assume that politicians decide what to do because there's an obvious 'best choice' option but in 1470 Warwick had no best choice left. The only solution to his difficult situation, the only way to protect his family and property, was to take the 'least bad choice': to depose Edward by restoring Henry VI and himself as Henry's chief councillor.

■ Should Warwick be a separate topic on the Success/ Failure line? If so, where would you place him?

Edward IV: success or failure?

The trouble with a conclusion such as 'Edward was a success' is that it's a generalisation, a brief statement summing up a complex issue as simply as possible. Generalisations are extremely useful, giving us a broad, approximate answer, but they miss out the nuances or subtleties of arguments. How does discussion of generalisations help with our enquiry into whether Professor Carpenter is right about Edward being a success despite losing his crown?

It helps because, to answer effectively, we have to go beyond a generalisation such as 'Edward IV was a success' or 'Edward was a failure'. To make an effective assessment of Edward's first reign we have to take into account that:

- Some aspects of Edward's rule were more successful than others. Your Success/Failure line probably shows a more complex picture than all successes or all failures.

- Edward did better at some times than at others, looking a success in 1465 but weaker in 1469.

- We can't assess Edward's actions just within the limits of the period 1461–69. We have to take into account the broader context. The situation Edward faced when he became king was very difficult (see diagram on page 76). This may make us assess Edward's kingship more positively.

- Some of the critical problems and events of 1468–69 were outside Edward's control: French support for Henry and Margaret, Warwick's decisions, Clarence's treachery. Not even kings are in control of everything.

All these points, especially the last two, help to explain Professor Carpenter's positive verdict on Edward. Yes, he was deposed and yes, he did make mistakes but Edward faced very considerable problems resulting from the events of the 1450s. These continuing problems, twinned with the unpredictable actions of Warwick, made Edward look vulnerable by 1468–9; in the view of historian A.J. Pollard, 'only marginally better than Henry VI'. However, if that was what people thought then they were very badly wrong. Edward was far better than Henry VI. Edward had a set of skills that he'd made little use of in the 1460s. In 1471 these military skills, as a leader and on the battlefield, were about to be unleashed on Warwick and the rest of Edward's enemies.

> The over-arching question in this book is about why war kept breaking out despite people's commitment to loyalty. What answers can you suggest for the outbreak of fighting in 1469–71?

■ Concluding your enquiry

Review your completed Success/Failure line and make sure you are confident in your placing of each topic. Now write your own assessment of Edward as king between 1461 and 1470, deciding how successful you think Edward was.

Is this the only book I should read?

NO! Never rely on just one book even if it claims it's the only book you need. Reading other books helps you develop deeper knowledge and understanding which is vital for success at A level. It also introduces you to other historians' views on individual topics and again this is important for success. Which other books should you read? Ideally not another book written just for A level but a book that takes you deeper. My favourite is John Gillingham's *The Wars of the Roses* (1981) because it is so interestingly written. It isn't up-to-date in terms of historians' debates but it'll give you a strong understanding of the pattern of events.

Another book I keep re-reading is Christine Carpenter's *The Wars of the Roses* (1997) because it makes me think and ask questions about interpretations I've taken for granted in the past. This enquiry on Edward IV is a good example, challenging the idea that Edward failed as king first time round. Edward's reputation has gone up and down over time. In the 1950s and 1960s historians were very positive about Edward's achievements but in 1974 Professor Ross wrote a detailed biography which was much more critical of Edward. Ross said Edward was inconsistent in his policies, too lenient to enemies, too generous to supporters, too inclined to rely on charm to win over opponents. Professor Carpenter's chapters on Edward are in part a response to Ross. In arguing that Edward was far more successful than Ross suggested, she particularly stresses the extent of the problems Edward faced on becoming king.

Therefore, when you read a history book, it's always important to know when it was written and so where it fits into a historical debate. Professor Carpenter's book, like any piece of historical writing, was written as part of a continuing debate among historians (see pages 10–11 for more on this idea). Try reading at least parts of her book yourself, not least because using an extract from a historian's book (as on page 77) is unfair as it risks simplifying or distorting his/her argument. One aim of this book is to give you confidence to move on to read and enjoy more demanding, detailed books and Professor Carpenter's book would be a good step up.

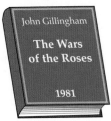

John Gillingham
The Wars of the Roses
1981

> Always check the author and date of a book. Is the book up-to-date with the latest debates amongst historians?

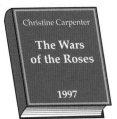

Christine Carpenter
The Wars of the Roses
1997

▷ Dame Fortune sits behind her wheel. This image and the idea of sudden, random turns of fortune that even affected kings was a familiar one in the fifteenth century. This picture comes from a book commissioned by William and Anne Herbert who you met on page 5. Until recently historians thought they gave the book to Edward IV but new research suggests they intended it for Henry VI as a gift around 1459, to make up for William's support for Richard of York. However, they never gave it to Henry – Dame Fortune's wheel turned against him and he lost his throne in 1461 before the book was completed.

The Yorkists
- Edward IV
- Richard, Duke of Gloucester
- Lord Hastings

Opposition to Edward IV
- Warwick
- Henry VI
- Margaret
- Prince Edward
- and Edward's own brother, George, Duke of Clarence

Pictures like this were often included in books for kings and nobles. Edward IV must often have seen them. They showed Dame Fortune turning her wheel, changing the lives of men and even kings from success to failure. In 1470–71 Edward IV himself went full circle, from triumph to disaster and back to triumph.

In September 1470 he lost his position as king on top of the wheel when he fled from Warwick's forces, escaping to Burgundy as a refugee. Warwick took Henry VI out of the Tower, dusted him off and made him king once more. But by May 1471, just eight months later, Edward was back on top, king again. Warwick, Henry VI and Prince Edward of Lancaster were all dead (killed or executed), crushed beneath Fortune's Wheel.

How did Edward turn the wheel in his favour? He used trickery, leadership and military skill, made the most of his enemies' disunity and had support from Burgundy. That support was vital but didn't come automatically. Late in 1470 the Duke of Burgundy needed English backing against France so he turned first to Warwick, who by then was ruling England in Henry's name. Only when Warwick allied with France did the Duke decide that he had to help Edward regain the crown as it was the only way he'd get English support.

Burgundy gave Edward £20,000, ships and facilities to prepare an invasion. When Edward set sail he might have been intercepted by Warwick's fleet but the commander, needing money to pay his men, was attacking trading ships.

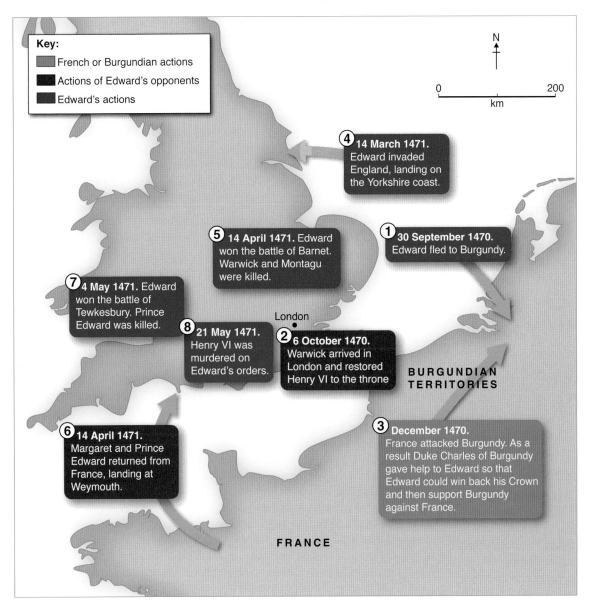

Key:
- French or Burgundian actions
- Actions of Edward's opponents
- Edward's actions

N

0 —————— 200
km

4 **14 March 1471.** Edward invaded England, landing on the Yorkshire coast.

5 **14 April 1471.** Edward won the battle of Barnet. Warwick and Montagu were killed.

1 **30 September 1470.** Edward fled to Burgundy.

7 **4 May 1471.** Edward won the battle of Tewkesbury. Prince Edward was killed.

London

8 **21 May 1471.** Henry VI was murdered on Edward's orders.

2 **6 October 1470.** Warwick arrived in London and restored Henry VI to the throne

BURGUNDIAN TERRITORIES

6 **14 April 1471.** Margaret and Prince Edward returned from France, landing at Weymouth.

3 **December 1470.** France attacked Burgundy. As a result Duke Charles of Burgundy gave help to Edward so that Edward could win back his Crown and then support Burgundy against France.

FRANCE

△ **The key stages of Edward's exile and return, 1470–71**

He might have been stopped by the French fleet but it was waiting to escort Margaret of Anjou to England. Storms did nearly stop Edward, scattering his ships before he landed in Yorkshire with just 500 men. Gradually other shiploads joined him until he had about 1200 men but there was no rush of Yorkshiremen to boost Edward's numbers. Hull refused to let in Edward and so did the city of York until, according to the chronicler John Warkworth, Edward announced that 'he was claiming only the duchy of York, his inheritance by right. He was not claiming the crown of England and before all the people he cried, "King Harry! King Harry and Prince Edward!"' (See pages 128–31 for more detail on Burgundy's attitude to and support for Edward.)

Edward's trickery worked. His army was fed and rested in York and then headed south. The Earl of Northumberland didn't stop him, probably because Edward had given him back his earldom in 1470. Montagu, though Warwick's brother, didn't stop him, realising his men would not fight Edward. And the further south Edward marched, the more people thought, 'they didn't stop him up north so why should we?' In the Midlands Edward unfurled the royal banner and announced he was back to be king. Men flooded to join him. His greatest gain was his brother George, Duke of Clarence who had been supporting Warwick. Now Clarence, bombarded with advice from his mother and sisters, begged Edward for forgiveness and switched back to fight for his brother.

By now it was also clear that Edward's opponents were deeply divided. The alliance between Warwick and Margaret had always looked unlikely but the divisions between them were making Edward's task easier:

- Margaret and Prince Edward were still in France. Margaret had not trusted Warwick enough to send over Prince Edward with Warwick, then bad weather delayed her.

- The Lancastrians didn't trust Warwick. Instead of uniting with Warwick to form one army to stop Edward, they preferred to join Margaret when she landed in the south west, thus splitting the forces facing Edward.

With Edward heading for London, his opponents paraded King Henry round the capital in a desperate bid to win support. The *Great Chronicle* tells how Henry was 'accompanied by the Archbishop of York, who held him by the hand all the way, and Lord Zouche, an old impotent man who bore the King's sword … this was more like a play than the showing of a prince to win men's hearts; for they lost many and won none or right few. He was showed in a long blue gown of velvet as though he had no more to change into.'

Unsurprisingly, no one rushed to support Henry and by now it was Edward who looked like the king. He rode unchallenged into London then turned to face Warwick's army. According to Edward's propaganda, his victory on 14 April at the battle of Barnet was largely the result of his own bravery for he 'manly, vigorously and valiantly assailed them in the midst and strongest of their battle and beat and bore down all that stood in his way'. However, *Warkworth's Chronicle* blamed confusion in Warwick's army because 'the Earl of Oxford's men had upon them their lord's livery [a star with streams] which was much like King Edward's livery, the sun with streams; and the mist was so thick that men could not tell one livery from another so the Earl of Warwick's men fought against the Earl of Oxford's men thinking they were King Edward's men. And the Earl of Oxford and his men cried "Treason!" and fled.'

Warwick and Montagu were killed but there was no rest for the victorious. Edward and his army headed west to deal with the Lancastrian half of his enemies, as Margaret had finally landed and met up with Somerset and the Lancastrian army. Edward caught them at Tewkesbury on 4 May. Again Edward and his young brother, Richard of Gloucester, led the hand-to-hand fighting. Prince Edward of Lancaster was killed and, on 21 May, Henry VI died too. According to Edward's propaganda, Henry died 'of pure displeasure and melancholy' on hearing the news of Tewkesbury. In fact he'd been murdered on Edward's orders. Edward was king again, thanks to Burgundy's help, his enemies' disunity, his own tactics and skills and because once he headed south he looked like the king again. He'd swung the momentum his way and the waverers had rushed to join him.

At Barnet, **Oxford** and Warwick were on the same side but Oxford was a loyal Lancastrian, a past enemy of Warwick; perhaps this encouraged fear of treachery

Henry VI was only 49 when he died. **Prince Edward** was 17

■ **Enquiry Focus:** Was Edward IV a success second time round?

This enquiry is very similar to the last one, investigating how successful Edward was, this time in his 'second reign'. It's often valuable to repeat a question because you can use what you've previously learned about how to tackle this type of question. The precise detail of the content will have changed but don't be fooled by that into thinking it's a completely different question. It's not. It's still asking you to make a judgement on the degree of Edward's success. Therefore, the kind of answer you're looking for and the vocabulary you use will be very similar.

1 The Success/Failure line again helps you collect evidence and reach your conclusion. Draw your own copy of the line. Use what you have learned about Edward to predict where each topic may go on the line. Pencil them in to create an initial hypothesis.

2 Think about the possible shape of your final answer. What does the pattern of topics suggest about the degree of Edward's overall success?

3 Read this enquiry. Remember to skim read first to get an overall sense of the material, then read it again carefully, placing each aspect of Edward's reign where you think it goes on the line. Make detailed notes to justify your choices and also note anything that makes the choice of placement difficult.

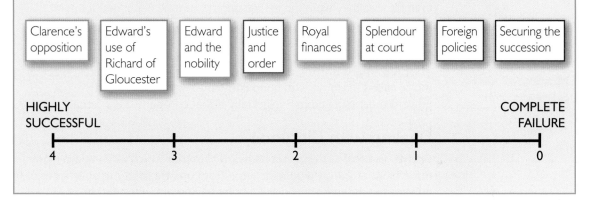

| Clarence's opposition | Edward's use of Richard of Gloucester | Edward and the nobility | Justice and order | Royal finances | Splendour at court | Foreign policies | Securing the succession |

HIGHLY SUCCESSFUL — 4 — 3 — 2 — 1 — 0 — COMPLETE FAILURE

Edward IV's style of kingship

Edward was only 29 in 1471, still a young man with the ability to charm his people. Dominic Mancini, an Italian visitor to London in 1483, recounted how, if Edward 'saw a newcomer [to court] bewildered at his appearance and royal magnificence, he would give him courage to speak by laying a kindly hand on his shoulder'. The *Great Chronicle* tells how Edward visited East Anglia to raise **benevolences** and 'handled the people so graciously that he got more money than he would have got from **two fifteenths**. It was reported that as he passed through a Suffolk town he asked a rich widow what she would contribute. She liberally granted him £10. He thanked her and then drew her to him and kissed her; which kiss pleased her so much that she gave £20 instead of £10.' Perhaps this wasn't surprising for a king who boasted of having three mistresses, 'the holiest, the merriest and the wiliest' in the whole kingdom.

After 1471 Edward faced a much easier political situation than he had in 1461. The deaths of Henry VI and Prince Edward removed the figureheads for opposition that had plagued him so much in his first reign. The distant Lancastrian heir was 14-year-old Henry, Earl of Richmond (also

benevolences
Payments to the king, said to be loans but really compulsory gifts

two fifteenths
A fifteenth was a tax. People in rural areas paid a fifteenth of the value of their movable goods. Townsmen paid a tenth

known as Henry Tudor). Although Henry was in exile in Brittany, his mother, Margaret Beaufort, was at Edward's court, negotiating for her son's return to take up his earldom. As Margaret's second husband had fought for Edward at Barnet it seemed likely that Henry would return to become a respected member of Edward's court. The remaining Lancastrian die-hards made peace with Edward. He even spared the lives of the Duke of Exeter and the Earl of Oxford who probably expected execution after fighting against Edward at Barnet. They were imprisoned, though Exeter was freed to join Edward's invasion of France in 1475.

However, Edward was not always charming. He was very conscious of his power, prepared to use his anger to over-awe individuals and bring them to heel. He was also very knowledgeable about his nobles and gentry. The royal official who wrote the continuation of the *Crowland Chronicle* knew the King and marvelled how Edward, though 'so fond of convivial company, debauchery, extravagance and sensual enjoyment, could have such a retentive memory that the names and circumstances of all men, scattered over the counties, were known to him just as if he were in the habit of seeing them daily'. Such knowledge of nobles and gentry was supremely important as they were the people upon whom he depended for good government in every part of his kingdom.

Overall, Edward combined cleverness and a capacity for hard work with a relaxed existence, to 'have all comfortable about him' in the words of Dr Rosemary Horrox. Edward's grandson, Henry VIII, wrote a piece of music called 'Pastime with good company', which was exactly what Edward most enjoyed too, especially if that company were female.

How might Edward's style of kingship have affected his chances of success as king after 1471?

Dealing with Clarence

George, Duke of Clarence was Edward's brother from hell, a quarrelsome, malevolent nuisance who ricocheted from one treachery to another until Edward put an end to his disloyalty by having him executed in 1478. Clarence's treachery had begun when he'd allied with Warwick against Edward and married Warwick's elder daughter, Isabel. He seemingly hoped that Warwick would make him king but Warwick put Henry VI on the throne, leaving Clarence no role in the Warwick–Lancaster alliance. Hence Clarence begged forgiveness of Edward, rejoining his brother in 1471. The word 'turncoat' scarcely does him justice.

Once Edward was king again, and with Clarence now proclaiming his loyalty, Edward planned to divide Warwick's lands between Clarence and their younger brother, Richard of Gloucester, but Clarence was not one for sharing. Knowing that Richard planned to marry Warwick's other daughter, Anne, and so secure his share of the Neville lands, Clarence had her kidnapped and hidden away (perhaps disguised as a kitchen maid) to stop the marriage. However, Clarence eventually had to give way at Edward's command. Gloucester married Anne and received Warwick's northern estates. Edward had needed the brothers to work together but instead there had been a very public quarrel.

The final crisis in their relationship followed the death of Isabel, Clarence's wife, in 1476. Although he seems to have genuinely grieved for his wife, Clarence soon had hopes of marrying Mary of Burgundy, one of the great heiresses of Europe. Edward refused to allow the marriage and

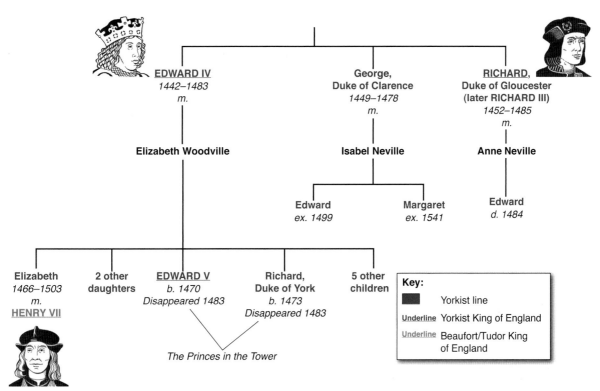

△ Edward IV's immediate family. The Yorkists were a thoughtless lot, using the names Edward and Richard far too often. Don't worry, you'll make sense of them after a while! Edward IV's eldest son, predictably another Edward, was born in 1470 after Edward had fled to Burgundy. The birth of his second son in 1473 added to the sense of greater security that the Yorkist line would continue.

also blocked a marriage with a Scottish princess. These decisions played their part in sparking Clarence's final tantrums. In April 1477 he sent armed men to arrest Ankarette Twynho, one his wife's former servants. In the space of a single day the poor woman was accused of poisoning Isabel, found guilty by a jury intimidated by Clarence's threats and then hanged. This was a huge abuse of power by Clarence. Then came what may have been a trumped-up charge, when a member of Clarence's household was convicted of using magic to forecast the King's death. Clarence defended his innocence at a royal council meeting in outright defiance of Edward.

Now Clarence himself was accused of treason, the culmination of a catalogue of offences that had finally broken Edward's patience. Clarence was put on trial at a Parliament specially called for the purpose, where Edward himself put the case against his brother. Clarence was found guilty and condemned to death. At that point Edward hesitated but finally ordered the sentence carried out. Clarence, only 28, was reportedly drowned in a barrel of malmsey wine. His death shows how determined Edward was to stop threats developing which would endanger his and England's security. It also shows, in the words of Dr Rosemary Horrox, 'the extent to which Edward was, by the late 1470s, master in his own kingdom'.

■ Place Edward's reaction to Clarence's opposition on your Success/Failure line.

Richard, Duke of Gloucester, the third brother

In some books you'll find that **Richard** is referred to as Gloucester, his title, and in others as Richard. Here he is called Gloucester while he is a duke, then Richard once he becomes king as Richard III in 1483

One effect of Clarence's treachery was to emphasise the loyalty of Edward's younger brother, Richard, Duke of Gloucester. Gloucester had gone into exile with Edward in 1470 and taken a leading role at Barnet and Tewkesbury, leading Edward's vanguard in hand-to-hand fighting, aged just 18. His reward was Edward's trust and widespread land and power in the north.

Before 1470 the north had created major problems for Edward because of Lancastrian invasions from Scotland and as the source of Warwick's power. Edward now solved the 'northern problem' by making Gloucester overlord of the region. Gloucester had spent several years in Warwick's household in the north during the 1460s but the picture below shows his key link with many northerners: his wife, Anne Neville, younger daughter of Warwick. Through Anne, Gloucester inherited Warwick's affinity, the widespread group of nobles and gentry whose loyalty was needed to defend the north against Scotland and maintain law and justice in the region. Although the initial loyalty of this group came through the marriage, events suggest that Gloucester's own character and treatment of individuals made that loyalty stronger.

Despite his northern powerbase, Richard of Gloucester was a national figure, acting as Constable and Admiral of England, leading the largest contingent in Edward's army in France in 1475 and leading the English army into Scotland in 1482. Such was his value to Edward that the King gave him the right to take possession of as much land in southern Scotland as he could capture and to rule it himself as a Palatinate, a semi-independent region under the English crown. For details of these campaigns see pages 100–101.

Edward and Richard of Gloucester made a powerful partnership, based on mutual support and self-interest. However, Gloucester's story was not only one of loyalty. He also showed a ruthless ability to further his own interests in clashes with Clarence, the Bishop of Durham and the Earl of Northumberland, in all of which he had Edward's support. He even used threats against the elderly Countess of Oxford when he wanted her lands in East Anglia. Gloucester threatened her with forcible removal to Yorkshire where 'the great journey and the great cold' would be the death of her. The Countess, a southerner, unsurprisingly gave way.

■ Place Edward's use of Richard of Gloucester on your Success/Failure line.

◁ Richard of Gloucester and Anne Neville portrayed after Richard became King Richard III in 1483. Anne had previously been briefly married to Prince Edward of Lancaster. She married Richard around 1473 and their only son, Edward, was born in 1476.

Edward and the nobility

Despite his problems with Clarence, Edward was well suited to managing and getting the best from his nobles. He understood that the most effective government was based on co-operation between king and nobles, making use of their desire for stability and order. The nobles respected his military skills, shared his enthusiasm for chivalry and appreciated his willingness to trust and involve them in government. Edward continued the policy he'd used before 1469 of using trusted supporters, especially members of the royal family, to control large regions (see map). These nobles were chosen for their effectiveness in maintaining royal control, not just their loyalty. Edward's deployment of these trusted noblemen gave him a control over the regions that he'd not possessed in his first reign.

A clear sign of Edward's approach after 1471 was his exclusion from local power of high-ranking individuals in order to increase royal authority. The best examples were Henry, Duke of Buckingham, married to a sister of the Queen and descended from Edward III, and also William Herbert, Earl of Pembroke, whose father had been Edward's most trusted supporter in Wales before being executed by Warwick in 1469. Both men lacked ability but still hoped to dominate Wales and the **Marches**. Instead Edward set up a Council in the name of his eldest son, the Prince of Wales, headed by the Queen's brother, Anthony Woodville, Earl Rivers and based at Ludlow. This gave Edward IV himself more direct control over the region.

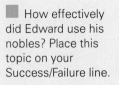 How effectively did Edward use his nobles? Place this topic on your Success/Failure line.

Marches
The borderlands between England and Wales

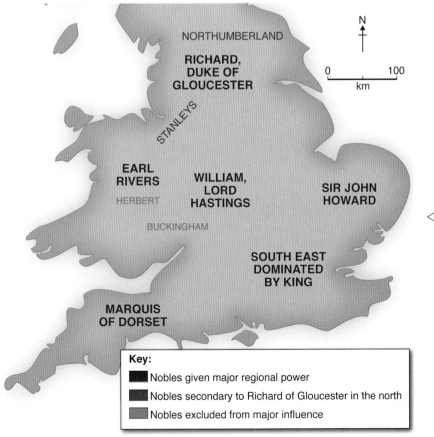

◁ This map shows the regions dominated by the men whom some historians have called Edward's 'super-nobles' (shown in red). From the mid-1470s they dominated their regions on Edward's behalf. Many less important nobles have been omitted for clarity.

Justice and order

Edward's use of his nobles as regional overlords played an important part in delivering justice. Equally important was his use of the network of gentry in every county. Many gentlemen developed links to Edward by becoming members of the royal household, taking up offices such as Knight or Esquire of the King's Body. These roles meant they were in close contact with the King for a part of each year, enabling the King to get to know them and a sense of trust to develop. The gentry then became the eyes and ears of the King in their counties, providing him with information and carrying out his commands.

However, there were weaknesses in Edward's policies. He was predominantly concerned with disorder that threatened political stability and his hold on the throne. For example, he stamped down on the dispute in the north west between the Harrington and Stanley families which threatened to disrupt the area. As a result, although the amount of lawlessness seems to have fallen, the Commons in Parliament did criticise his failure to punish 'such persons as either be of great might or else favoured by persons of great power'. It's possible that Edward paid less attention to run-of-the-mill crime or disorder initiated by his trusted nobles.

Royal finances

Edward's improving financial situation was one of his successes. He benefited from the up-turn in trade and agriculture, thereby gaining greater income from customs duties and from his estates. He also increased income from royal estates through more efficient administration by his officials. Edward also exploited royal rights more effectively, increasing income from wardships, for example. A ward was the heir to a nobleman's estate but too young to take over the lands. While the heir was a child, the King had the right to income from the estates in return for supervising his/her upbringing. Alternatively he could sell the wardship to another nobleman and take money for arranging the heir's marriage.

The most controversial of Edward's financial arrangements was the extraction of benevolences, 'gifts' of money from a subject to the King. This might appear very civilised but there was little possibility of someone's refusing to make a 'gift' to the King, especially in the run-up to an invasion of France. However, it's a sign of Edward's greater security after 1471 that benevolences, while resented, did not lead to widespread complaint and rebellion.

Wealth did not affect Edward's security as king but it did raise his status in the eyes of his people. His wealth created the impression of a king who was financially competent, making the best of his own income and certainly not wasteful, one of the criticisms of Henry VI. This perception of competence may, in turn, have encouraged Parliament to agree to taxation, expecting it to be used efficiently.

■ Place the three topics on these pages on your Success/Failure line.

Having read these pages, review where you have placed Edward's use of his nobility.

Splendour at court

What did Edward spend his income on? A clear idea comes from the *Crowland Chronicle*, with an eye-witness account of the royal Christmas celebrations in 1482, when Edward 'dressed in a variety of the costliest clothes very different in style from what had been seen before. The sleeves of his robe hung full and the insides were lined with sumptuous fur, displaying the King (whose elegant figure always stood out) like a new and incomparable spectacle before the onlookers. This was a royal court befitting a mighty kingdom …'

As the writer suggests, Edward's expenditure was neither frivolous nor selfish. A king needed to look magnificent to embody his kingdom's strength and wealth. Edward had been well aware of this before his exile and was even more so afterwards, having seen the splendour of the Burgundian court, the most sumptuous in Europe.

Major occasions were celebrated with grand jousts. Edward and his family and courtiers showed off the richest clothes and jewellery, ate off the finest plate, employed the best musicians. Edward also spent lavishly on the finest craftsmanship, especially in his rebuilding of his favourite palaces, Fotheringhay and Nottingham in the Midlands and Eltham, Windsor and Greenwich near London. At Nottingham he built a new polygonal tower with 'marvellous fair' windows and chambers, described by John Leland in the 1500s as 'the most beautifullest and gallant building for lodging … an exceeding fair piece of work'. However, the greatest of his buildings was the new chapel of St George at Windsor, shown below.

◁ St George's Chapel, Windsor. This breathtakingly beautiful building, where Edward was buried, was the supreme artistic achievement of his kingship.

Foreign policies

If you ever go into St George's Chapel at Windsor, kneel down and look under the seats in the choir! There you'll find beautiful wooden carvings called misericords. One of them portrays a controversial moment during Edward's reign, showing his meeting with Louis XI of France at Picquigny in 1475. What was so controversial about a meeting between kings? It was peaceful, when the English people, including Edward's own brother, Richard of Gloucester, had expected war. This was the second time Edward had made peace, not war, with France. He'd planned an invasion in 1468, raised taxes to pay for it, but then abandoned the plans. So in 1475, when he again collected taxes, people expected a real and glorious war, especially as Edward had had robes made for his coronation ceremony as king of France and had made alliances with Burgundy and Brittany to combine their strength against France.

But, when Edward led his army (the largest so far in the 1400s) across the Channel in July 1475, there were no battles. Burgundy and Brittany failed to provide the promised support, leaving Edward isolated. Thus, Edward met Louis at Picquigny to agree a treaty. The terms included a seven-year truce, marriage between the **Dauphin** and Edward's eldest daughter, and a large payment by France to Edward, a bribe to take his army home. He received £15,000 immediately and then £10,000 per year. His soldiers were bribed too, with large quantities of alcohol, and they caroused their way round the streets before falling fast asleep in the gutters.

> The **Dauphin** was the title of the heir to the French crown

Why did Edward agree to peace? He clearly believed a war without Burgundian support was both too risky and, since it was likely to be long-lasting, extremely expensive. He had also gained a good deal financially through the treaty, perhaps more than if he'd fought a campaign, and he'd united his nobles and gentry in a military enterprise. Although the demobbed soldiers again let their alcoholic habits loose on their return to England, the expedition may have made England more peaceful for a period. Financially it was certainly a good policy. Edward didn't collect any unpaid taxes earmarked for the French campaign and didn't collect tax again until 1482. Thus, the invasion was a practical success if not a glorious one.

Edward's other major foreign concern was Scotland. By 1480 Scottish attacks over the border, culminating in a large-scale raid into north-east England, were becoming more than a nuisance. Therefore, in 1481 Edward planned a major campaign to punish the Scots with himself in command. That campaign was abandoned but quickly replaced by one led by Richard of Gloucester in 1482. The aim was to depose King James III, making James' brother, the Duke of Albany, king instead. Albany was happy to agree to hand over Scottish territory to England in exchange for the crown. Gloucester captured the border fortress of Berwick and led his army into Edinburgh but at that point the royal Scottish brothers made peace with each other. Gloucester withdrew southwards but kept Berwick. The campaign was good for Gloucester's reputation and his relationship with his affinity (many of whom were knighted on the campaign). Most importantly, it warned off the Scots from raids in the immediate future. There were criticisms, however. The *Crowland Chronicle* called the capture of Berwick 'a trifling gain, or perhaps more accurately, loss (for the maintenance of Berwick costs £10,000 a year)', which 'diminished the wealth of the King and the kingdom by more than £100,000. King Edward was grieved at the frivolous expenditure of so much money …'

The Scottish campaign also caused a wider problem. Edward, preoccupied with Scotland, could not provide help when Burgundy sought English aid to invade France. Eventually Burgundy abandoned England and agreed a treaty with France. As a result France scrapped her treaty with England! The plan for the Dauphin to marry Edward's daughter was abandoned and France stopped paying Edward his £10,000 a year! Therefore, by 1483, Edward had protected his northern border but had gained little in Europe. Did that matter? No; as long as there were no threats of invasion, and there weren't. Edward's policies may not have been glorious but neither had they undermined his security.

> ■ Place Edward's foreign policy on your Success/Failure line. Should France and Scotland go in the same place?

Securing the succession, but what happened next?

The years after 1478 were the most stable of Edward's reign. By March 1483 he appeared to have done everything needed to ensure a smooth succession for his heir. Edward, Prince of Wales, was aged 12 and there was a 'spare' son (Richard of York) should illness strike young Edward. As Edward IV himself was only 40 it was very likely that his son would be a young man at least before becoming king.

What happened next has created one of the major debates about the extent of Edward IV's success. Edward died on 9 April 1483. He'd been ill for only a couple of weeks and his death was clearly a surprise as key individuals, including Prince Edward (the Prince of Wales) and Richard of Gloucester, had not had time to return to London. But then, instead of Prince Edward's smooth succession as Edward V, within three months Edward V was deposed by Richard of Gloucester, he and his younger brother disappeared and several major nobles were executed.

Was this turmoil Edward IV's fault? Should he have foreseen what was to happen and taken steps to prevent it? Professor Christine Carpenter argues that Edward, 'one of the greatest of English kings', was not to blame. He left 'his dynasty securely settled on the throne' and in her view no one could have predicted Richard of Gloucester's actions. Other historians, however, definitely blame Edward for the deposition of his son. They say he had:

- given too much power to individual nobles, notably Richard of Gloucester; power that was used to depose young Edward V
- allowed enmities to grow and fester, particularly involving the Queen's family (the Woodvilles). Once Edward was dead, these feuds exploded into violence with individuals putting enmities before their loyalty to the young king. (See page 103 for details of these enmities.)

The weakness in this critical viewpoint is hindsight, assuming that these enmities must have been visible before Edward IV died. In contrast, Dr Rosemary Horrox, in her book *Richard III: A study of service*, made a thorough review of the evidence, concluding: 'the evidence [for enmities] is so slight that it implies that any animosities had been held in check by Edward IV and only surfaced fully after his death. The speed with which they then became an issue, however, shows that they were real enough.'

This suggests that Edward was very much the master of his kingdom in 1483 and that his authority prevented enmities flaring into anything greater. One final point: if we look ahead to early June 1483, only weeks before young Edward was deposed, it's clear that nobody expected this to happen. His coronation was being planned. Nobles at the centre of events were completely unaware of what lay round the corner. Therefore, it seems very harsh to blame Edward for not foreseeing the danger to his son when nobody foresaw it even two weeks before it happened. As we'll see in Chapter 7, what happened between April and July 1483 astonished everyone in the country.

■ Concluding your enquiry

1 After reading the section headed 'Securing the succession' and page 103, place 'Securing the succession' on your Success/Failure line.

2 Review the placement of all the topics on your line now that you have read the whole enquiry.

3 Consider reading other books on Edward IV to compare their conclusions with those in this enquiry.

4 Write up your own judgement on the extent of Edward's success, using your Success/Failure line to help you. Also think about the following:

  a) Which aspects of kingship were most important to people at the time? Should you give extra weight to these aspects in assessing Edward's success?

  b) Context: did Edward face an easier task as king after 1471 than he had in his first reign? Does this affect your conclusion?

  c) Should Edward be blamed for not anticipating and preventing what happened after his death?

The importance of dates

Many people think dates are a nuisance, 'facts' to be learned to show that you know them 'for the sake of knowing them'. But dates are far more important than that! They're like the letters of the alphabet. Letters aren't much use on their own but combined into a pattern they become words. Dates too become really important when part of a pattern with other dates. Dates help us to put events in the right sequence – and they tell us how long the gaps were between events. There's a really important example in the next chapter when knowing the dates, and so the duration of time between them, helps us to understand what was happening. As you'll discover, Richard of Gloucester arrested Earl Rivers and then had Hastings executed but note the dates: the first event was on 30 April, the second on 13 June – there's over 6 weeks in between. Without the dates we wouldn't see there was such a long gap between these events and we wouldn't ask important questions such as 'Why was there such a long gap?' and 'What does this gap tell us about Richard's plans?' That's why dates are important: they help us to ask questions, then to understand what was happening and to explain those events more effectively.

At the death-bed of Edward IV

This diagram sums up the relationships between leading figures at the time of Edward's death. It supports the contention by Dr Horrox that the evidence for enmities is very limited, with the hostility between Hastings and Dorset the one obvious rivalry.

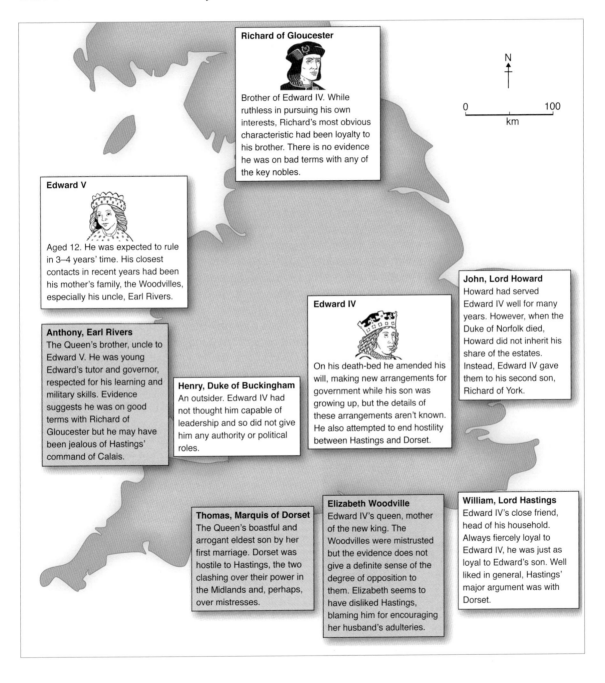

Richard of Gloucester

Brother of Edward IV. While ruthless in pursuing his own interests, Richard's most obvious characteristic had been loyalty to his brother. There is no evidence he was on bad terms with any of the key nobles.

N

0   100
km

Edward V

Aged 12. He was expected to rule in 3–4 years' time. His closest contacts in recent years had been his mother's family, the Woodvilles, especially his uncle, Earl Rivers.

John, Lord Howard
Howard had served Edward IV well for many years. However, when the Duke of Norfolk died, Howard did not inherit his share of the estates. Instead, Edward IV gave them to his second son, Richard of York.

Edward IV

On his death-bed he amended his will, making new arrangements for government while his son was growing up, but the details of these arrangements aren't known. He also attempted to end hostility between Hastings and Dorset.

Anthony, Earl Rivers
The Queen's brother, uncle to Edward V. He was young Edward's tutor and governor, respected for his learning and military skills. Evidence suggests he was on good terms with Richard of Gloucester but he may have been jealous of Hastings' command of Calais.

Henry, Duke of Buckingham
An outsider. Edward IV had not thought him capable of leadership and so did not give him any authority or political roles.

Thomas, Marquis of Dorset
The Queen's boastful and arrogant eldest son by her first marriage. Dorset was hostile to Hastings, the two clashing over their power in the Midlands and, perhaps, over mistresses.

Elizabeth Woodville
Edward IV's queen, mother of the new king. The Woodvilles were mistrusted but the evidence does not give a definite sense of the degree of opposition to them. Elizabeth seems to have disliked Hastings, blaming him for encouraging her husband's adulteries.

William, Lord Hastings
Edward IV's close friend, head of his household. Always fiercely loyal to Edward IV, he was just as loyal to Edward's son. Well liked in general, Hastings' major argument was with Dorset.

How certain can we be about why Richard III took the crown?

Northampton, 29 April 1483

It was a good evening, according to the sources – laughter, cheerful conversation, a good meal. Three men enjoyed that evening. One was Anthony, Earl Rivers, uncle of the new king, Edward V. Rivers was escorting 12-year-old Edward from Ludlow to London for his coronation. Edward was staying in nearby Stony Stratford that night.

> **Rivers**, aged 41, was brother of Elizabeth Woodville, Edward V's mother
>
> **Richard, Duke of Gloucester**, aged 30, was Edward IV's brother
>
> **Buckingham** was 28

The second man was Richard, Duke of Gloucester. Gloucester and Rivers had known each other for years, had fought alongside each other to win back Edward IV's throne, and shared a deep religious piety and enthusiasm for chivalry and crusading. The third man, Henry, Duke of Buckingham, was the outsider. He had played little part in Edward IV's government. Edward apparently doubted Buckingham's abilities and never gave him responsibility.

The three men said good-night, agreeing to ride together next morning to meet the King. What actually happened shocked everyone, except Gloucester and Buckingham.

Next morning they arrested Rivers, then more members of the King's household, including Richard Grey, the King's half-brother. Rivers and Grey were sent north as prisoners. Two months later, they were executed on Gloucester's orders. Next day, 26 June, Gloucester was proclaimed king as Richard III.

Edward V's reign had lasted less than three months. The boy had not died and yet now his uncle Richard was king. Did Richard of Gloucester have the crown in mind that evening two months earlier as he sat talking cheerfully with Rivers and Buckingham? This chapter explores what may have led Richard to take the crown.

◁ Richard, Duke of Gloucester, Richard III. Portraits from the 1500s show Richard as a thin-faced, slim, wiry figure, but as most portraits were copied from others the similarities are not surprising! He is also shown fidgeting with his ring, a habit echoed in descriptions of his constantly pulling his dagger half way from its sheath and putting it back. This may have been a real habit or a later invention of hostile witnesses trying to show a restless, anxious personality.

What happened in the spring of 1483?

The beginning	
9 April	Edward IV died. His 12-year-old son, now Edward V, was at Ludlow on the Welsh border. He was supervised by Anthony, Earl Rivers. Edward IV's brother, Richard, Duke of Gloucester was on his lands in Yorkshire.
Mid-April	The coronation was set for 4 May. Councillors headed by Lord Hastings told Rivers to limit King Edward's escort to London to 2000 men. Hastings and Buckingham were in communication with Gloucester.
The first shock	
29 April	Rivers met Gloucester and Buckingham at Northampton over dinner.
30 April	Gloucester arrested Rivers and took control of Edward V. Rivers and Richard Grey were sent north as prisoners.
	When the news reached London, the King's mother, Elizabeth Woodville, and her other children fled to sanctuary in Westminster Abbey.
4 May	Edward V arrived in London, accompanied by Gloucester and Buckingham.
Early May	The Council appointed Gloucester as Protector until Edward V was old enough to rule. Edward was lodged in the royal apartments in the Tower of London to prepare for his coronation, now set for 25 June.
The second shock	
13 June	William, Lord Hastings was executed without trial on Gloucester's orders. Gloucester said Hastings had plotted treason against him.
16 June	Gloucester sent the Archbishop of Canterbury and a band of armed men to Elizabeth Woodville in sanctuary in Westminster. They persuaded her to allow her second son to join Edward V in the Tower. The coronation was postponed again.
25 June	Rivers and Grey were executed at Pontefract in Yorkshire.
Richard's crown	
26 June	A petition was presented to Gloucester, asking him to become king. It said that Edward IV's children were illegitimate because he had made a pre-contract of marriage with another woman before he married Elizabeth Woodville.
6 July	Richard of Gloucester was crowned King Richard III.

Who's Who? (Check the family trees on pages 81 and 95.)

- Richard, Duke of Gloucester (Richard III) – Edward IV's brother, powerful landowner in the north
- Edward V and Richard, Duke of York – Edward IV's sons
- Elizabeth Woodville – wife of Edward IV, mother of Edward V and his brother
- The Woodvilles – relatives of Elizabeth Woodville, including her brother, Anthony, Earl Rivers, and her two sons by her first marriage, Thomas, Marquis of Dorset and Richard Grey
- William, Lord Hastings – Edward IV's closest friend and chamberlain (head) of his household
- Duke of Buckingham – related to the royal family but given little power and authority by Edward IV

■ **Enquiry Focus:** How certain can we be about why Richard III took the crown?

Richard III's reign is full of puzzles we don't have definite answers for, including why he took the crown. So, instead of pretending we can be definite, this enquiry explores how far we can go along the line towards certainty about Richard's motives.

Certain motives	Probable motives	Possible motives	Unlikely motives

1 Create a copy of the Certainty line above, then pencil in each of the motives below where you currently think it may go on the line.

2 Make a list of possible reasons why we might not be certain about Richard's motives.

3 Use your answers to 1 and 2 to sketch out a short paragraph answering the question.

4 Read pages 106–11 fairly quickly. Don't try to take in all the details but get an overview of the main issues and ideas. Then read it again slowly, tackling the activities as you go. This 'double-layer' of reading is by far the most effective way to study.

> **Richard, Duke of Gloucester**
> (Richard III) was the son of Richard, Duke of York, killed at Wakefield in 1460. They were two different people! Try not to confuse the two Richards!

The range of motives suggested by historians to explain Richard's actions

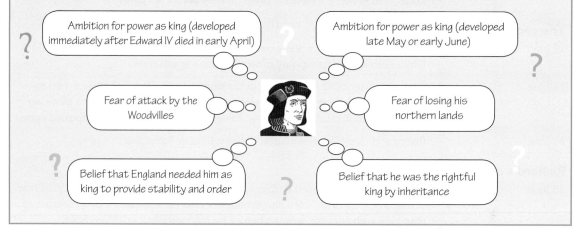

? Ambition for power as king (developed immediately after Edward IV died in early April)

? Ambition for power as king (developed late May or early June)

Fear of attack by the Woodvilles

Fear of losing his northern lands

? Belief that England needed him as king to provide stability and order

? Belief that he was the rightful king by inheritance

Analysing Richard's motives

Ambition for power as king (developed immediately after Edward IV died in early April)

■ Where would you place the motive 'ambition for power in early April' on the Certainty line?

Many writers have assumed that Richard was motivated by ambition for power but it's unlikely that he wanted the crown as soon as he heard of Edward IV's death. If he had wanted the crown from the beginning then he'd probably have taken action to become king far sooner than mid-June. Instead, events unfolded slowly. The Council appointed Richard as Protector. The administration of government continued normally with few changes in personnel. Edward IV's household men (headed by Hastings) supported Richard as Protector. It was 'government as before' through May and into June, with six whole weeks between the arrest of Rivers on 30 April and the execution of Hastings on 13 June – six weeks with no sign of Richard's wanting the crown. This strongly suggests that Richard was not ambitious for power the moment Edward IV died.

A reminder: who were the Woodvilles?

(See the Woodville family diagram on page 81.)

They were the family of Elizabeth Woodville, Edward IV's queen and Edward V's mother. In 1483 the leading family members were the Marquis of Dorset (her elder son by her first marriage) and her brothers, Anthony, Earl Rivers and Sir Edward Woodville, an admiral who took his ships to sea when he heard Richard had arrested Rivers. The Woodvilles were influential, thanks to Elizabeth being Queen and their dominating Edward V's council when he was Prince of Wales, but they were not powerful, lacking large numbers of retainers to fight for them. This made them vulnerable to Richard's armed support.

Fear of attack by the Woodvilles

Richard twice said his actions were driven by Woodville threats to his life and power. He justified the arrest of Rivers and Grey in late April by claiming they were plotting to stop him taking a leading part in the young King's council. Then later, on 10 June, he wrote to the city of York:

> Right trusty and well-beloved … we heartily pray you to come unto us in London as speedily as possible after the sight of this letter with as many well-armed men as possible, to aid and assist us against the Queen, her blood and other adherents and affinity who intend to murder and utterly destroy us and our cousin, the Duke of Buckingham and the old royal blood of this realm.

Was Richard really threatened by the Woodvilles or was this a cover story, a plea of self-defence, aiming to win support by pinning the blame on the Woodvilles?

◁ This illustration shows Anthony, Earl Rivers presenting a copy of the *Dictes of the Philosophers*, which he had translated, to Edward IV. To the right of the King are Queen Elizabeth Woodville and Prince Edward, later Edward V.

First, did the Woodvilles want to stop Richard playing a leading role in the council? Almost certainly, yes. The best evidence comes from the *Crowland Chronicle's* history of the Yorkist kings written early in 1486. We don't know the name of that writer but the details included suggest he was a well-informed government official, often an eye-witness to events. He wrote how 'the more foresighted members of the Council … thought that the Queen's family should be absolutely forbidden to have control of the young king until he came of age.' This implies that the Woodvilles wanted to dominate Edward V's government instead of there being a broad council including Richard.

So the Woodvilles threatened Richard's place at the centre of power, even if it's unlikely they threatened his life or lands at this first stage. There was no previous hostility between them. A month earlier Rivers had asked Richard to arbitrate in a legal dispute. Rivers really was taken by surprise when arrested by a man he thought was a friend. It is possible, however, that Richard was heavily influenced by Buckingham and Hastings. They were both in contact with him in April and Hastings in particular had rivalries with members of the Woodville family.

Second, did the Woodvilles plan to 'murder and utterly destroy' Richard? If they did, we must look at Richard's his own actions: arresting Rivers and later, as Protector, taking many of the Woodvilles' lands and positions and giving much of their wealth to Buckingham. These actions created a real enmity between Richard and the Woodvilles, symbolised by Elizabeth Woodville and her children (except Edward V) living in sanctuary in Westminster Abbey. By early June Richard must have realised the significance of this enmity. He could be Protector for only four years at most. Then Edward V would rule and almost certainly recall his Woodville relatives to positions of power from which they could take revenge on Richard. His strike for the crown in June was probably more prompted by what the Woodvilles might do in the future, in revenge for his actions, than by fear of what they were doing at that time, especially as in 1483 they had far less armed power and support than Richard.

<aside>
■ Where would you place the motive 'fear of the Woodvilles' on the Certainty line?
</aside>

Fear of losing his northern lands

No contemporary writer mentions this motive and it wasn't one that Richard could give in public but it may have been important. It's a motive deduced by historians who have pieced together individual pieces of information. Richard's possession of his vast northern territory wasn't permanently secure. It had been granted to Richard by his brother, Edward IV, and could be taken away. In particular his hold on parts of the former Neville family land was vulnerable. The 'real' heir to these Neville lands was George, Duke of Bedford (see family tree, right) but Bedford couldn't inherit because his father had been attainted for treason. While Bedford (and any children of his) were alive, the attainder stayed in force, so Richard kept the lands and could pass them on to his son. But on 4 May 1483 Bedford died without children, ending the attainder and changing Richard's hold on this land. He would keep it until he died but then it would go to the next Neville heir, one of the Latimers, not to Richard's son.

<aside>
■ Where would you place the motive 'fear of losing his northern lands' on the Certainty line? What links can you suggest between this and other possible motives?
</aside>

What could Richard do about this? He could safeguard his lands while he was Protector but his Protectorate would end in four years at most. Then the Woodvilles would be back in power. Then he could well lose much

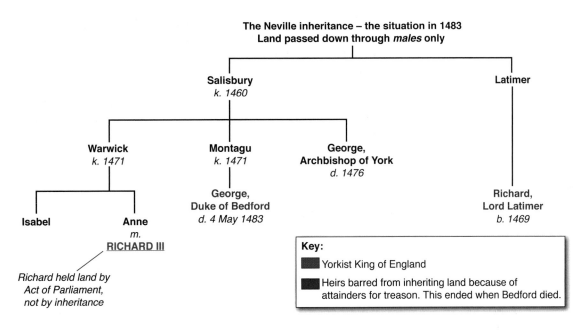

or all of his land by order of the young Woodville-dominated King. So was Richard motivated to take the crown to safeguard his lands? Without Richard's own words we have no evidence for this but it's a possible motive at least. It would become more probable if Richard hadn't heard of Bedford's death until late May or early June; this would make sense of the sudden rush of events and his ruthless execution of Hastings.

△ This family tree shows the links between George, Duke of Bedford and the Latimers.

Belief that he was the rightful king by inheritance

In 1484 Parliament approved Richard's right to be king in a document called *Titulus Regius*:

> At the time of the contract of the marriage [between Edward IV and Elizabeth Woodville] King Edward was and stood married and troth-pledged to one Dame Eleanor Butler, daughter of the old Earl of Shrewsbury, with whom King Edward had made a pre-contract of marriage … it follows evidently that King Edward and Elizabeth lived together sinfully and damnably in adultery and that all children of King Edward are bastards unable to inherit ….

This was the justification circulated by Richard in June 1483. He said that he was the rightful king because everyone more closely related to Edward IV was barred from the throne, either by illegitimacy (Edward's children) or by Act of Attainder for treason (Clarence's son).

Did Richard believe that his nephews were illegitimate, and so believe that he was rightfully king, or had he faked the story as a legal excuse for taking the crown? There are strong arguments for its being fake. Its appearance out of the blue at an extraordinarily convenient moment raises suspicion. More importantly, bastardy need not have stopped Edward V becoming king because the coronation would have wiped out illegitimacy (as it did later with Queen Elizabeth I). Richard ignored this possibility, which suggests his priority was his own power and position. Finally, people's reactions suggest widespread doubt about the story. The best informed contemporary writer, the Crowland chronicler clearly didn't believe a word:

> Richard, the Protector, claimed the kingdom for himself. The pretext for this was … put forward in a certain parchment roll that King Edward's sons were bastards because he had been pre-contracted to a certain Lady Eleanor Butler before he married Queen Elizabeth … It was put about then that this roll originated in the north whence so many people came to London although there was no one who did not know the identity of the author (who was in London all the time) of such sedition and infamy

Look at the chronicler's choice of words: 'pretext' meaning pretence or alleged reason and 'sedition and infamy' meaning treason and evil. It's true the author often shows hostility to Richard but that's because he believed that Richard had no justification for taking the crown. He was not the only person. Later in 1483 many gentry rebelled against Richard because they did not believe in his right to be king. Richard did not convince them at the time. It's hard to see why he should convince us today, but equally we cannot be certain the story is untrue. Without access to Richard's thoughts we can't know for sure.

■ Where would you place the motive 'belief in being rightful king' on the Certainty line?

Belief that England needed him

Another motive suggested by historians but not mentioned by contemporaries is that Richard may have been motivated by a sense of duty. In the 1450s, his father the Duke of York had been convinced England needed him to end the political crisis (see page 43). Perhaps Richard also saw himself as the man for a crisis, guiding England through the potential problems of Edward V's minority, using his experience as a general, as a powerful landowner and as Edward IV's trusted brother. His own published claim to the throne emphasised his devotion to the common good and to righting past failures. Such a sense of duty would fit with his deep religious faith and serious approach to government as king. It may help explain his determination to be Protector and perhaps his decision to take the crown. Equally he must have known that deposing Edward V would lead to instability and perhaps rebellion, the very opposite of the stability England needed.

■ Where would you place the motive 'belief that England needed him' on the Certainty line?

Ambition for power as king (developed late May or early June)

It seems that Richard had decided to take the crown by 10 June, when he wrote to the city of York for armed support. Did he make this decision simply out of the desire to be king? Richard has often been portrayed as motivated by power because of the ruthlessness with which he seized the crown. William, Lord Hastings, Edward IV's closest friend and utterly loyal to Edward's son, would not countenance Richard becoming king. On 13 June Richard had Hastings arrested and executed without trial, all in a matter of hours. A fortnight later Rivers and Grey were executed, again without proper trial. The shock of this violence silenced potential opposition. It certainly looked as if he were solely interested in power, but behind these actions probably lay either fear of Woodville revenge and the loss of his northern lands or the belief that he was the rightful king and a sense of duty.

Why is certainty so difficult?

We have identified a range of motives but it is very difficult to be certain about which ones dominated Richard's thinking. Why is it so difficult?

- Accounts written by others are of limited value as they couldn't see into Richard's mind.

- Richard's own public explanations have to be questioned because he needed to present the explanation most likely to win support.

- Motives change over time. Three months of dramatic events may have seen Richard's motives change. We all know from our own experience, of making up our minds about something complicated, that different factors jostle for dominance in our minds and swap around in significance.

- We don't know whether he was thinking rationally throughout or whether he panicked at times, taking one bad decision (the arrest of Rivers) before stumbling into an even worse one (taking the crown).

In addition, explanations of Richard's motives will be affected by our view of:

- Richard's career as a whole. If we focus on his loyalty to his brother then we're more likely to accept that he believed in the illegitimacy story; if we focus on his ruthlessness we're more likely to emphasise ambition for power and defence of his northern lands.

- Richard's character. Was Richard a natural leader, the driving force behind events or, as Professor Christine Carpenter has suggested, a born second-in-command who could be manipulated, first by Hastings, then by Buckingham?

- The period as a whole. If we see the fifteenth century as a time when actions were primarily motivated by ambition then Richard's motives will fit that pattern, but if we identify idealism as a possible motive then perhaps Richard was at least partly driven by a sense of duty.

We could spend many more pages discussing this issue, without altering the fact that we don't know exactly what motivated Richard. You may wonder why we've spent so long on a topic where there's such lack of certainty, but that's the whole point. Too often people assume that History is all about finding the 'right' answer, when most of the time we actually identify only degrees of certainty, with probabilities and possibilities rather than complete certainty. Hopefully this enquiry will have helped deepen your understanding of these issues and you've realised the fascination of uncertainty!

> ■ Where would you place the motive 'ambition to be king in May/June' on the Certainty line? What links can you suggest between this and other possible motives?

■ Concluding your enquiry

Review the positions of each motive on your Certainty line and then revise your original hypothesis in answer to the enquiry question.

Why was Richard able to take the crown?

■ Read your other books to build up a detailed answer to the question in the heading, using the diagram as a guide.

Why Richard took the crown isn't the only question to ask about these events. Equally important is why he was able to become king. Plenty of people later rebelled against him, so why didn't anyone stop him in June 1483? There isn't space to explore this question in detail so the diagram opposite sums up the reasons why Richard was able to take the crown.

At the heart of the explanation is that Richard's strike for the crown took everyone by surprise. Even on 16 June, three days after Hastings' execution, Elizabeth Woodville sent her second son to join his brother, Edward V, to prepare for Edward's coronation in the royal apartments in the Tower. This seems totally inexplicable if she had the faintest idea that Richard intended to take the crown. Both Rivers and Hastings had also been taken completely by surprise. Richard's actions were continually beyond anyone's expectations.

Powerful support was also critical to Richard's success. Hastings' support (or at least his opposition to the Woodvilles) made it much easier for Richard to become Protector, the stepping-stone to the crown. Richard also had support from Buckingham and probably from John, Lord Howard. Howard had hoped to inherit lands from the Duke of Norfolk but Edward IV gave them to his younger son. This may have led Howard to back Richard. As soon as Richard was king he made Howard Duke of Norfolk. And, in the critical weeks in June, Richard was strongly backed by the threat of force. News of his summoning a northern 'army' on 10 June spread round London. By the time the northerners arrived, the crown was Richard's but the threat of their arrival had played its part.

The impending **arrival of Richard's northerners** must have sparked memories of the threat from Margaret of Anjou's northerners in 1461. See page 66

△ These signatures, Edward V, Richard of Gloucester and the Duke of Buckingham, were apparently jotted down during Edward V's journey to London. Above Richard's signature is his motto 'Loyaulte me lie' (Loyalty binds me). Richard's emphasis on loyalty is used by some to argue that he must have believed that Edward was illegitimate or he would not have deposed his brother's son. But amidst the fast-moving events of mid-June such ideals may have taken second place to fear and the need to react to events.

SURPRISE

■ Richard's past loyalty to Edward IV

In 1470 Richard had joined Edward in exile when Clarence sided with Warwick. Since 1471 he had been completely loyal, leading Edward's army against Scotland and controlling the north of England. No one, least of all Rivers and Hastings, expected him to depose his brother's son.

■ His moderate actions in May and early June

Until mid-June Richard took every opportunity to stress his loyalty to Edward V. As Protector he gave no sign of wanting greater power.

■ The violence of his actions in mid-June

On 13 June Hastings was executed. Other potential opponents were arrested and imprisoned. This unexpected violence paralysed potential opposition. Only days earlier, Hastings had been saying how well things were going, that the overthrow of the Woodvilles had been achieved 'with only as much bloodshed as would come from a cut finger'.

■ The speed of events in mid-June

After six weeks of calm came ten days of frantic action, at the end of which government went quiet while everyone waited for Richard to be crowned. There was no time to organise effective opposition.

STRENGTHS

■ Support from significant noblemen

Hastings played a critical part in Richard's becoming Protector. Buckingham and Howard backed his claim to be king, adding credibility and perhaps making potential opponents hesitate.

■ His northern support

Rumours of the arrival of Richard's northern army alarmed Londoners and intimidated potential opponents.

■ The weakness of potential opponents

The Woodvilles had little power. The arrest of Rivers killed any chance of their leading opposition to Richard. Other major nobles were too preoccupied with their own concerns over their positions under a child-king that they did not unite against Richard.

UNCERTAINTIES OF POTENTIAL OPPONENTS

■ A justification for becoming king

The story of the illegitimacy of Edward's children probably made many potential opponents pause. Was it true? Before they decided, Richard was king. This claim also gave waverers an excuse for supporting him.

■ Memories of the minority of Henry VI

People remembered the bad days of Henry VI and many blamed this on his long **minority**, unaware that problems had only begun once Henry was an adult. Therefore, uncertainty over what might happen under another boy king perhaps played into Richard's hands.

■ Confusion

A letter from Simon Stallworth to Sir William Stonor, written in London on 21 June, sums up the confusion. Amongst the news he says, 'there is much trouble and every man doubts the other …' This confusion about what was really happening made it difficult to rally opposition to Richard.

minority
The state of not yet being an adult. There was no set age when a monarch's minority ended. Henry VI began ruling at 16 but the age varied according to the individual and could be as low as 14

'The most untrue creature living'

Grantham, Lincolnshire, 12 October 1483

Richard III had been king for only three months but already a major rebellion was developing across the south of England. The letter opposite gives us a remarkable glimpse into Richard's mind as he planned how to deal with the rebels. Richard was not surprised by the rebellion, as his informers had been very efficient, but he was shocked by the involvement of the Duke of Buckingham, his closest supporter when he'd taken the crown.

What's remarkable about the letter, sending shivers up my spine whenever I look at it, is that larger handwriting is Richard III's handwriting, a direct link to one autumn day over 500 years ago. The core letter, written by his secretary, asks the Chancellor, Bishop Russell, to send the Great Seal to Richard so he can use it to authenticate his orders. Then Richard picked up a pen himself. He writes a few lines, urging Russell to send the Great Seal as swiftly as possible, and then his anger at Buckingham bursts out, beginning near the end of the penultimate line below the original letter. In modernised spelling it reads:

> Here, loved be God, is all well and truly determined and for to resist the malice of him that had best cause to be true the Duke of Buckingham the most untrue creature living, whom with God's grace we shall not be long till that we will be in those parts and subdue his malice. We assure you was never false traitor better purveyed for, as the bearer, **Gloucester** shall show you.

Gloucester was Richard's herald

Richard sounds confident that Buckingham's fate is sealed, 'never was false traitor better purveyed [provided] for', but you can feel the intensity of his anger at Buckingham in the words 'him that had best cause to be true' and in his description of Buckingham as 'the most untrue creature living'.

Henry Stafford, Duke of Buckingham (1455–83)

Buckingham is a mystery. He married Catherine, one of Elizabeth Woodville's sisters, but after he returned early from Edward's IV's French campaign in 1475 he played no part in political life. Edward gave him no responsibilities, which suggests Edward didn't trust or rate him. Then Buckingham suddenly re-appeared in 1483, constantly alongside Richard of Gloucester as he became Richard III. What was Buckingham's motive? Was he bitter about being married off to a Woodville when he may have hoped to marry one of Warwick's daughters who would have brought him more land? Was he bitter about being left out of politics? Richard gave him huge areas of land and authority in Wales, the west Midlands and the south west, far more than is logical for a man Edward IV hadn't rated. But then Buckingham joined the rebellion against Richard. Why? Had he wanted even more reward? Was he involved, as some rumours said, in the deaths of the Princes? Did he think that he could become king? We don't know. Buckingham is very much a mystery.

8 Was Richard III defeated because of the disappearance of the Princes?

It was the fate of the Princes in the Tower that first got me interested in the Wars of the Roses. Many years ago my eye was caught by a book cover showing a face that turned out to be Richard III. The book was Josephine Tey's *The Daughter of Time*, a 'whodunit' exploring whether the Princes were really murdered by Richard III. The sense of mystery is created because there are no trustworthy sources telling us directly what happened to the Princes. At best, writers imply what happened. Take Dominic Mancini, an Italian in London in 1483, who seems to have information from Edward V's doctor:

Edward V and his brother, Richard of York, were aged 12 and 9 in June 1483

> … all the King's servants were barred from access to him. He and his brother were withdrawn into the inner rooms of the Tower and day by day began to be seen more rarely behind the windows and bars, until they ceased to be seen altogether. The physician, Argentine, the last of his attendants, reported that the young king, like a victim prepared for sacrifice, made daily confession and penance because he believed that death was facing him.

The inference is that the boys died in summer 1483 but there's no detail of how they died. In addition, Mancini spoke no English, so was dependent on what others told him, and he wrote several months later, when it was widely believed the boys were dead. Mancini may simply have been telling the story people expected to hear.

All the sources have similar problems, so there is no trustworthy document telling us what happened. However, a different kind of evidence exists in the actions of those who rebelled against Richard in autumn 1483. What's significant is the identity of those rebels. The great majority had been loyal followers of Edward IV, so this was a Yorkist rebellion aiming to put Edward V back on the throne. But then they changed their plan, deciding to support Henry, Earl of Richmond (Henry Tudor). This was a remarkable change. Hardly anyone knew Henry. He'd been in exile since 1471, had no training for kingship and only the remotest claim to the throne and that was through the Lancastrian line (see page 119). The only explanation for these loyal Yorkists backing the Lancastrian heir is that they believed Edward V and his brother were dead. They would not have turned to Henry if they'd believed the Princes were alive.

These men's actions provide the most compelling evidence that the Princes were dead. They clearly believed that Richard was responsible and this belief led them to rebel, then go into exile with Henry and finally to return to defeat Richard. However, was the disappearance of the Princes the sole reason for Richard's defeat or did other factors play an even greater part?

116

■ **Enquiry Focus:** Was Richard III defeated because of the disappearance of the Princes?

This enquiry isn't just about the disappearance of the Princes. It explores other factors contributing to Richard's defeat, their significance and whether they were linked to the Princes' disappearance.

1 As you read this enquiry, build up a causation diagram like the one below which shows the factors involved in Richard's defeat. After the discussion of each factor, annotate your diagram and make supporting notes using these questions as a guide:

- Was the factor linked to the disappearance of the Princes? If so, how?
- What links can you see to other factors?
- How was the factor linked to his defeat?
- How important was this factor in Richard's defeat?

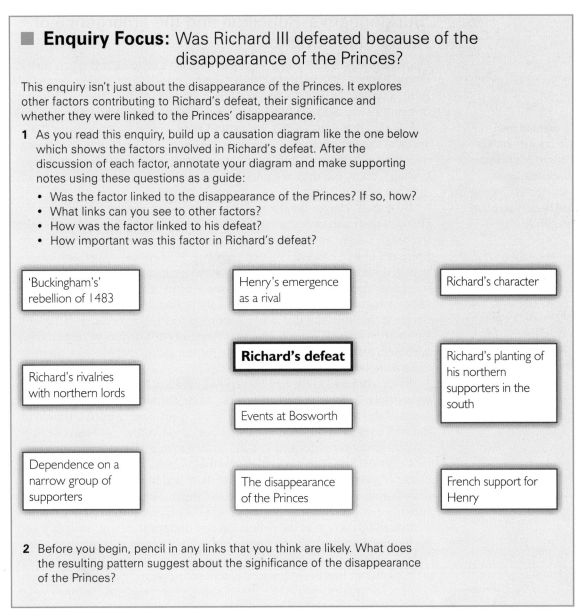

'Buckingham's' rebellion of 1483

Henry's emergence as a rival

Richard's character

Richard's defeat

Richard's rivalries with northern lords

Richard's planting of his northern supporters in the south

Events at Bosworth

Dependence on a narrow group of supporters

The disappearance of the Princes

French support for Henry

2 Before you begin, pencil in any links that you think are likely. What does the resulting pattern suggest about the significance of the disappearance of the Princes?

What do we call Henry Tudor?

This seems a daft question. The man who became Henry VII is usually called Henry Tudor before 1485 and Tudor is one of the most famous names in history. The trouble is Henry didn't use the name Tudor. He called himself by his title, Henry, Earl of Richmond. Richard III called him Tudor in public proclamations as an insult, to draw attention to Henry's descent from Owen Tudor, an obscure Welsh squire. Very unroyal! And, as the historian C.S.L. Davies has shown, people in the 1500s didn't use the name Tudor or write about 'the Tudors'. The kings and queens didn't call themselves Tudors. So, to be polite to Henry, this book mostly calls him Henry of Richmond!

'Buckingham's' Rebellion and the emergence of Henry of Richmond

Opposition began in the first weeks of Richard's reign. There was a plot to rescue Edward IV's daughters from sanctuary and an attempt to rescue the Princes under cover of outbreaks of fires around London. The involvement of John Cheney, Edward IV's Master of the Horse and standard bearer, was a clear sign that Edward IV's **household men** were recovering from the shock of the execution of their leader, Hastings. Richard had hoped these men would be the core of his support, demonstrating continuity from his brother's reign, but they regarded him as a usurper and were prepared to fight to restore Edward V.

By August a larger rebellion was being planned but the rebels soon changed their aim of restoring Edward V. Believing the Princes to be dead, the rebels sought an alternative candidate for the crown. They might have preferred one of Edward IV's nephews but, for a variety of reasons (too young; under Richard's control), they were unsuitable. Their choice, the inexperienced Henry of Richmond, was second best but he did have a connection to the crown through the Lancastrian line. However, don't be deceived into thinking this was a Lancastrian rebellion because of Tudor's Lancastrian links. It wasn't. This was fundamentally a Yorkist rebellion with Henry the new Yorkist candidate for the crown. For Henry's claim to the crown, see the family tree opposite.

By October 1483 rebellion had spread right across the south. How many were involved we don't know, but what made the rebellion a threat was the status of the rebels: leading gentry in nearly every county from Cornwall in the west to Kent in the east. Their motives varied. A few had been out of political favour for years and saw the chance to ingratiate themselves with a new ruler (Henry). The Woodvilles and their relatives were involved, unsurprisingly given their loss of power, land and the executions and disappearances they'd suffered. However, the majority of rebels had not suffered demotions or loss of land or authority under Richard. They were motivated by outrage at the deposition and disappearance of Edward V and his brother. Contrary to what people today often assume, the murder of children was seen as just as great a crime in the 1400s as it is now. Kings had been deposed before but never a child-king and never an adult king who hadn't caused serious problems for many years. These rebels had a great deal to lose – lives, families, wealth – yet they risked rebellion in a moral protest against Richard's behaviour, persuading others to rebel through family links or friendship.

◁ A sketch of Henry of Richmond (Tudor) as a young man. (See page 139 for his upbringing before 1471.) In 1471, when Edward IV returned, Henry had been taken to live in Brittany by his uncle, Jasper Tudor. Henry's ambition had been to return to England to take his place amongst the nobility. Instead, the disappearance of the Princes turned him into a candidate to be king. As the autumn rebellion unfolded, it's likely that Henry's mother, Margaret Beaufort, and John Morton, Bishop of Ely, made contact with Elizabeth Woodville and others, pushing Henry into the minds of the Yorkist rebels as a possible leader.

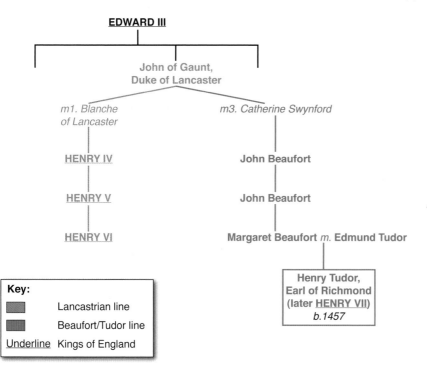

EDWARD III

John of Gaunt,
Duke of Lancaster

m1. Blanche
of Lancaster

m3. Catherine Swynford

HENRY IV

John Beaufort

HENRY V

John Beaufort

HENRY VI

Margaret Beaufort *m.* Edmund Tudor

Henry Tudor,
Earl of Richmond
(later HENRY VII)
b.1457

Key:

▉	Lancastrian line
▉	Beaufort/Tudor line
<u>Underline</u>	Kings of England

◁ A simplified family tree showing Henry of Richmond's claim to the crown through his mother, Margaret Beaufort, and his link back to Edward III. See also the family tree on page 38

Yet the rebellion failed dismally. One reason was the extreme difficulty of co-ordinating a rising across the whole of the south. Some rebels took no decisive action, waiting for others to join them. Second, Richard was well prepared, warned by his spies of what was happening. Third, some potential rebels didn't join in, which brings us to the role of Buckingham whose name is often misleadingly given to the rebellion even though he did not join until very late on.

The most likely reason for Buckingham's joining the rebellion is that he expected Richard to be overthrown and so deserted what he thought was Richard's sinking ship. But rats can drown! His arrival weakened the rebellion. Until then, the rebels had hoped for support from the powerful Talbot and Stanley families. When Buckingham joined the rebellion, it seems that these families, rivals of Buckingham in north Wales and the Welsh border, decided to stay out. For them, one of the attractions of the rebellion was taking Buckingham's land, so they weren't going to fight on his side!

By the time Henry's ships neared the coast, the rebellion had failed. Buckingham was executed. Henry sailed back to Brittany where he was joined by around 400 rebels. Others returned to their homes with no option but to make their peace with Richard. But the rebellion, despite its failure, did affect Richard's chances of keeping the crown:

- It established Henry as a rival for the crown. At Christmas 1483 he promised to marry Edward IV's eldest daughter, Elizabeth of York, another clear sign that he was the Yorkist candidate for the crown.

- The flight of rebels to Brittany gave Henry a core group of supporters, men who'd been leaders in their counties, such as John Cheney and Giles Daubeney. Many of those who stayed in England would follow these men if they returned at the head of an invasion.

▉ How strongly was the rebellion linked to the disappearance of the Princes?

How did the rebellion weaken Richard?

What impact did Henry of Richmond's emergence as leader have on Richard's position?

Complete your diagram for these factors.

The planting of northerners in the south

Richard had defeated the rebellion but it left him with a major problem. A significant number of rebels had fled abroad. They were the men who made local government work in their counties, by acting as judges in county courts, as sheriffs, as members of commissions into major crime or treason or by raising defence forces when needed. Now there were gaps in this network in almost every southern county. In addition, could Richard trust the gentry still in England, the friends and neighbours of the rebels?

Richard had to fill these gaps. His solution was to use men from his own affinity (mostly northerners with whom he'd built up a close relationship since the 1470s). At first he chose to fill the gaps with men who already had connections in the south. For example, in Kent his first choice was Ralph Ashton from Lancashire who had married a Kentishwoman, Elizabeth Kyriel, earlier in 1483 and so had land in Kent. Ashton was given significant rewards of land, responsibility for investigating rebels' possessions, and other posts. However, there were not enough such northerners with links with Kent, so Richard had to import complete outsiders, who were given local authority and lands. Kent became the new base for Robert Brackenbury from Durham, Ralph Bygot, Marmaduke Constable and William Mauleverer, all from Yorkshire, and several other northern gentry.

This pattern was repeated in many southern counties. The result was pockets of northern newcomers in every county. Their presence aroused great hostility, as voiced by the author of the *Crowland Chronicle*:

> [Richard] distributed all these [lands] amongst his northerners whom he had planted in every part of his dominions, to the shame of all the southern people who … longed more each day for the return of their old lords in place of the tyranny of the present ones.

'Tyranny' is a harsh word to use. Was the arrival of the northerners really so terrible? Although there is no evidence of physical intimidation by the newcomers, their arrival was deeply shocking to the local gentry. The gentry in each county made up a close-knit community, intermarried with long-standing friendships, used to working together. Now they had two, three or more outsiders in their county, men they saw as Richard's spies and resented for taking over the lands of local friends or relatives. These outsiders had been imposed on the locals without any regard for their reactions, hence the sense of tyranny.

So Richard's 'planting' of northerners created great resentment in the south. This was a long way from the continuity in government that he'd hoped for when he intended to use Edward IV's household as his core supporters. The planting demonstrates that Richard was not in control of events. The violence used in taking the crown and the disappearance of the Princes had led to rebellion and then rebellion had led to the planting of northerners and this, in turn, increased the chances of more rebellion. Richard was having to react, to make second-best choices, hoping they wouldn't make his situation worse. This was not a recipe for success.

■ To which other factors is the planting linked?

Was there a link back from the planting to the disappearance of the Princes?

Complete your diagram for this factor.

The effigy of Edward Redmayn and his wife Elizabeth, above, dating from *c.*1510, can be seen in the church at Harewood in West Yorkshire. Edward Redmayn was one of the northerners whose lives changed dramatically in 1483. Edward, a lawyer, played the same roles as other gentry in Richard's affinity in the 1470s and early 1480s. For example, in 1483 he sat on the Commissions of the Peace in the West Riding and Westmoreland (where his family had lands) and on commissions to assess taxes. So far, so ordinary.

Then came the rebellion in October 1483. Edward was summoned south with other northerners to arrest rebels in Devon and Cornwall. Over the next 18 months he was given considerable authority in the south west, sitting on commissions to array defence forces in Dorset and Wiltshire, to deal with crime in Wiltshire, and to investigate treasons in Devon. He was appointed Sheriff of Somerset and Devon in 1484. His rewards included lands forfeited by local rebels.

Thus, the man in the photograph was one of the northerners whom the *Crowland Chronicle* said were so hated. One thing we can't know is what this experience was like for men such as Edward, knowing his presence in the south was resented by the locals.

Another question is 'what did Edward think of Richard III?' Many people regarded Richard as a usurper who had stolen his nephew's crown. Yet there were as many, especially in the north, who were deeply loyal to Richard (see also page 126). This loyalty seems to have been based on far more than self-interest. Many probably thought Richard would be a genuinely good king, a man whose qualities and character had won their loyalty. Edward was probably one of them though we cannot know.

After Bosworth, Edward returned north. He lost the lands in the south but was pardoned by Henry VII and eventually restored to authority in the north, becoming Sheriff of Cumberland in 1492. He was back to the life of an ordinary northern gentleman, carrying out routine tasks alongside others who had briefly been catapulted south by Richard III's need for loyal supporters.

Richard's rivalries with northern lords

Richard had dominated the north since the early 1470s, building up a loyal affinity. However, two leading families felt threatened by Richard's dominance. The first was the Stanley family, headed by brothers Lord Thomas and Sir William, whose lands were mostly in Lancashire and Cheshire. They had clashed with Richard since 1469, especially over the Stanleys' fight with the Harrington family for possession of Hornby Castle. Richard's support for the Harringtons, who were members of his affinity, infuriated the Stanleys, although Edward IV intervened to end any chances of fighting. Once king however, Richard was eager to settle the argument in the Harringtons' favour, giving the Stanleys a reason to fight against Richard. In addition, Thomas Stanley's wife was Margaret Beaufort, mother of Henry of Richmond!

> ▇ At first this factor doesn't seem to have any links to the Princes, but does it?
>
> Complete your diagram for this factor.

Why should I support Richard when he gives Lincoln my place in the north?

Northumberland

Why should we support Richard when he favours the Harringtons?

Lord Thomas Stanley

We would gain more when your step-son, Henry, is king.

Sir William Stanley

The second northerner was Henry Percy, Earl of Northumberland, another who had reluctantly taken second place to Richard's dominance. Once Richard became king, Northumberland hoped to be the leading power in the north, only to find that Richard promoted his nephew, the Earl of Lincoln, an outsider to the region, a clear sign that Richard would maintain his close involvement in the north. If Henry of Richmond invaded, could Richard depend on Northumberland's loyalty?

Dependence on a narrow group of supporters

Richard had good intentions as king. He was particularly interested in the legal system and his only Parliament (in 1484) made reforms to ensure everyone had access to justice, especially those who could not afford lawyers. He worked hard at public order and royal finances, helped by the fact that the government bureaucracy kept running smoothly. However, efficiency could not counter-balance Richard's failure to provide stability, the most important element of kingship. Threats of rebellion never went away, leading him to ever greater dependence on a small core of supporters.

We have seen several times that the accusation of ruling through a small, unrepresentative group of 'favourites' was very damaging. In 1450 this was a major accusation against Suffolk. In 1469 Warwick criticised Edward IV for allowing the Woodvilles too much influence and in 1483 Richard himself claimed he was saving England from dominance by a Woodville clique. But by 1484 Richard had been forced into the same trap, summarised by William Collingbourne's rhyme:

> The Cat, the Rat and Lovell our Dog,
> Rule all England under a Hog.

> **Collingbourne** was executed in 1484, not for terrible poetry but for treason: plotting against Richard

The Hog was Richard, after his badge, the white boar. The advisers in the first line were William Catesby, Richard Ratcliffe and Francis, Lord Lovell. Other members of Richard's inner circle were Robert Brackenbury, James Tyrell and John Howard, who was made Duke of Norfolk by Richard. All were highly rewarded. Ratcliffe, for example, received a rich haul of lands in Devon but such rewards only created another problem. If any rebels wanted to return from Brittany, Richard had no lands to give them or else he had to take them back from his supporters.

Richard had not intended to be dependent on this small group but the events of May–June 1483 and the autumn rebellion had forced this situation on him. Richard did try to deal with the problem. When a trickle of rebels returned to England in 1484, they were pardoned. Most dramatically, Richard persuaded Elizabeth Woodville to come out of sanctuary and take her place at court with her daughters. This was great propaganda for Richard, sending the message, 'if Elizabeth Woodville is at Richard's court then she can't think Henry has much chance of success'. This is also one of the most intriguing

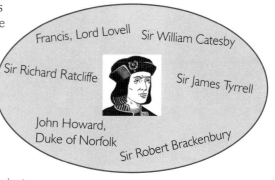

Francis, Lord Lovell   Sir William Catesby
Sir Richard Ratcliffe   Sir James Tyrrell
John Howard, Duke of Norfolk   Sir Robert Brackenbury

moments of this period. Why did Elizabeth appear at court if Richard had murdered her sons? The most likely solution is that she was playing both sides for the good of her surviving family. If Henry's threat waned, she had to make peace with Richard at some point but her eldest daughter, Elizabeth of York, was still promised in marriage to Henry.

Then, in March 1485, came the news that Richard's wife, Anne Neville, had died, followed by the rumour that Richard now intended to marry Elizabeth of York, his niece. Other rumours said that Richard had poisoned Anne so that he could marry Elizabeth, thus stopping her marrying Henry and so diminishing his claim to be Edward IV's natural successor. These rumours were so strong and unpopular that, according to the *Crowland Chronicle*, Richard's closest advisers, Ratcliffe and Catesby, 'told the King to his face that if he did not deny [this rumour] the northerners … would all rise up against him …'

Richard did make public denials, a humiliating thing for a king to do, but these rumours tell us several things:

- Richard's reputation was so bad after the disappearance of the princes that people could believe he would poison his wife.

- He was so heavily dependent on his northern support (which he'd first gained through his marriage to Anne Neville; see page 96) that they could threaten to abandon him.

- He was so desperate to end the combined York–Woodville–Beaufort–Tudor threat that marriage to his niece was even considered.

To which other factors is Richard's dependence on a small number of supporters linked?

Can you trace a link between this factor and the disappearance of the Princes?

Complete your diagram for this factor.

Richard's only son died in 1484 and his wife in 1485. Without an heir there was now no continuity and, though Richard was young, it would be at least 15 years before a new-born son would be adult. Could this have made men wonder if Richard was worth supporting? Should these deaths be a factor on your causation diagram?

△ Elizabeth of York, eldest daughter of Edward IV and Elizabeth Woodville. She was aged 17 at Christmas 1483 when it was agreed that she would marry Henry of Richmond, cementing the anti-Richard alliance. She married Henry after Bosworth and went on to be the mother of Henry VIII.

Henry failed in 1483 but succeeded in 1485. To what extent can this difference be explained by French aid?

Complete your diagram for this factor.

French support for Henry of Richmond

Foreign policy was another area where Richard was forced to react rather than pursue the policies he'd have chosen if free from rebellion. He saw himself as a warrior-king, ideally waging war against Scotland and France. However, instead of invading Scotland he was forced to reach a truce in 1484, because of the death of his only son at Easter and because it was an expense he couldn't afford owing to the need to be ready to combat an invasion.

That invasion looked increasingly threatening by 1485 because of events in France and Brittany. Brittany was an independent dukedom and the Duke wanted English aid for his fight to retain independence from France. This had led to a marriage arrangement between Edward V and Anne of Brittany, the Duke's daughter. The Duke must have been alarmed at the disappearance of Edward V but he still began negotiations with Richard for English help. What could Brittany offer Richard in return? Brittany could hand over Henry of Richmond.

At this point both French and Breton politics became complicated by internal rivalries but the result was that Henry fled from Brittany to France to avoid being handed over to Richard. Henry was welcomed in France because the government was concerned that Richard might attack France. Thus, France supported Henry in order to distract Richard from launching an invasion.

The news that France was supporting Henry encouraged a number of defections from Richard to Henry late in 1484. The English garrison of Hammes Castle, near Calais, defected to Henry, taking with them one of the few remaining Lancastrian nobles, the Earl of Oxford. Even more importantly, France provided Henry with practical military help: a fleet of ships to transport around 4000 soldiers, including over 2000 French soldiers and 1000 Scots from the King of France's guard. These numbers are estimates but show the importance of French aid.

Events at Bosworth, 22 August 1485

What Richard needed, the only thing that might provide stability, was complete victory over Henry and the exiled Yorkists. Thus, when Richard heard that Henry had landed in Pembrokeshire on 7 August, 'he rejoiced,' according to the *Crowland Chronicle*, 'saying the day he had longed for had arrived'.

Henry's invasion force can best be described as an anti-Richard alliance of former members of Edward IV's household, French and Scots soldiers, and a handful of former Lancastrians, notably the Earl of Oxford. As he marched into England his force grew, increased by men such as Walter Hungerford and Thomas Bourchier, who'd rebelled in 1483 and now saw a second chance to defeat Richard. Summoned to fight for Richard, they slipped away to join Henry.

Despite the increase in Henry's army, Richard had the larger force when the two armies met near Bosworth in Leicestershire on 22 August (see page 4). The Stanley forces were near by. Richard had tried to ensure they didn't join Henry by taking Lord Stanley's son as a hostage. As with other battles, it's hard to reconstruct what happened that morning. Henry's vanguard, led by Oxford, may have had the advantage in early fighting but Richard nearly won. His cavalry charge at the head of his household knights brought him close enough to exchange blows with Henry before Sir William Stanley's force intervened and Richard was killed. One puzzling feature is the failure of the Earl of Northumberland's men to join the battle on Richard's side (or Henry's). Did he deliberately betray Richard, angry at Richard's failure to give him control in the north or did he simply have no opportunity because Richard charged much sooner than expected, leaving Northumberland to watch events unfold?

Richard was killed. So too were most of his closest supporters, including Norfolk, Ratcliffe and Brackenbury. Even Polydore Vergil, writing later for Henry, praised Richard's bravery, saying he was killed 'fighting manfully in the thickest press of his enemies'. Henry of Richmond (Henry Tudor), who'd had no expectations of the crown three years earlier, was now King Henry VII.

> ■ To which factors do the events at Bosworth link back?
>
> Was Richard's defeat certain before the battle?

◁ Historians have argued for many years over the exact location of the battlefield of Bosworth. Archaeological surveys finally led to the identification in 2010 of the core of the battlefield, marked by finds of cannonballs (such as those shown here).

Other finds from the battlefield include this ▷ silver-gilt boar, Richard III's badge, probably a prized possession of a member of his affinity who died at Bosworth.

The character of Richard III

Occasionally, amidst the politics, we can catch a glimpse of the man, not the king. When Richard's only legitimate son, Edward, died in April 1484, the *Crowland Chronicle* provides a poignant description of the King and Queen 'almost out of their minds for a long time when faced with this sudden grief'.

Other glimpses can be found in people's behaviour. One northerner, William Mauleverer, proudly left in his will 'a little ring with a diamond that King Richard gave me'. This suggests, along with other evidence, Richard's ability to inspire great loyalty amongst his affinity. Richard is the only king of England to have a strong connection with the north. While his 'northern-ness' can be exaggerated, since he was always a national political figure, he spent much time in the 1470s at his castle of Middleham in North Yorkshire. He planned to build a chantry in York for 100 priests, which suggests he wished to be buried in York, the strongest evidence of his affection for the north. That affection was returned, at least by some. When news of Richard's death reached the city of York its ruling council recorded, 'King Richard, late mercifully reigning over us … was piteously slain and murdered to the great heaviness [sorrow] of this city.' It is deeply puzzling how one man could inspire such loyalty in some and yet such hostility in others.

The great variety of reactions to Richard helps make his character hard to define. Yet again we have to be cautious, but perhaps one character trait relevant to his defeat was impulsiveness. At key moments in his reign Richard seems to have acted with great suddenness and perhaps without enough thought, creating problems for himself which only grew greater with time. The arrest of Rivers was the first, then the execution of Hastings and the seizure of the crown and finally his last charge at Bosworth. All perhaps had arguments in their favour, arguments which seemed good at the time, but they turned out to be mistakes. If it had not been for Richard's impulsiveness in 1483, England would have been spared over two years of uncertainty, a rebellion and an invasion, and the Wars of the Roses would have ended in 1471.

> ■ Can you trace a link between this factor and the disappearance of the princes?
>
> Complete your diagram for this factor.

Was Richard III defeated because of the disappearance of the Princes? Some points to think about

Richard made success very difficult for himself. Having become Protector, claiming to represent continuity from his brother, he then destroyed that continuity with his deposition of Edward V. His hopes that his brother's household would become the heart of his support then disappeared when they rebelled after the disappearance of the Princes. The rebellion then led him to plant his own supporters in the south, creating further opposition. His dependence on a narrow group of supporters, dominated by his own northern affinity, was just the kind of narrowly based government he'd claimed to oppose in 1483 when he took action against the Woodvilles. The disappearance of the Princes even fuelled the French belief that Richard was an aggressive king who planned an invasion of France, and there's no doubt that French support played a major part in Henry of Richmond's success.

So, was Richard doomed by the disappearance of the Princes? Not quite! If the disappearance of the Princes had been the key to defeat then perhaps Richard would have been toppled by the 1483 rebellion. Secondly, in 1485 if events within France had gone differently, France might not have supported Henry, leaving Henry stranded without support for an invasion. Thirdly, Richard could have won at Bosworth. If William Stanley's charge had been delayed by another minute or two then Richard might have killed Henry and ended the battle in victory. Success at Bosworth would then have given him the chance to establish himself, plus the ability to claim God's approval for his victory. In that case Richard, over time, might have emerged as a very capable king (he was only 32 when he died).

But Richard lost at Bosworth and, though French support for Henry was a very significant factor, Henry would never have become his rival but for the way Richard took the crown and the widespread belief that he was responsible for the deaths of the Princes. So great was the opposition to Richard that Professor Christine Carpenter has suggested that, even if Henry had been killed at Bosworth, members of Edward IV's former household would have found another candidate to oppose Richard, perhaps one of the de la Pole family, sons of a sister of Edward IV and Richard III.

■ Concluding your enquiry

1   Revise your causation diagram, identifying links between factors.

2   Place each factor on your own version of the diagram below in order to identify the relative significance of the factors in Richard's defeat. Use your completed causation diagram to help you.

3   Write an answer to the enquiry question. Which of these phrases most sums up your conclusion?

'To a great extent Richard was defeated because of the disappearance ...'

'This was only one factor amongst several ...'

'The disappearance of the Princes played a part but was less important than ...'

'The disappearance of the Princes was insignificant compared with ...'

'This factor was the most important because it led to other events that ...'

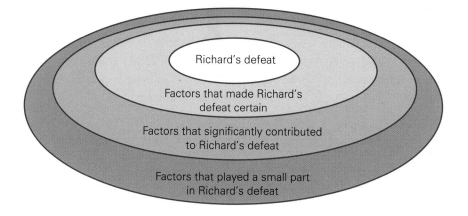

Richard's defeat

Factors that made Richard's defeat certain

Factors that significantly contributed to Richard's defeat

Factors that played a small part in Richard's defeat

9 How influential was the role of other countries in the Wars of the Roses?

'King by the grace of Charles VIII' is one verdict on Henry of Richmond's victory at Bosworth, meaning he owed his Crown to the King of France. If we add Scots' support for Lancastrian invasions after 1461, French help to restore Henry VI in 1470, and Burgundian assistance to Edward IV in 1471, it seems as if other countries played a very significant part in the wars. This enquiry investigates how true this is.

■ **Enquiry Focus:** How influential was the role of other countries in the Wars of the Roses?

Page 88 discussed the strengths and weaknesses of generalisations. This enquiry asks you to develop a more effective, more complex answer to the question above than this generalisation:

Other countries played a very significant part in the wars.

1   First jot down your thoughts on how accurate this statement is. Your work so far should enable you to think of examples of foreign involvement and how influential they were. Then draft your own answer in a short paragraph.

2   To build up a good answer, we need to investigate three sub-questions (see a–c) in relation to each of these five periods:

   1455   1459–61   1461–64   1469–71   1483–85

   To do this, read pages 129–31, look back at earlier enquiries and use other books for more information.

a. What kinds of foreign involvement took place?

For each period above, find out what kinds of foreign involvement took place. Did they provide:

Military aid   Diplomatic assistance

Refuge   Transport

b. Why did other countries involve themselves in English politics?

For each period above, find out why foreign involvement took place. Some possibilities are:

Self-defence   Existing alliances
Trading advantages   Family links
Desire to destabilise the English king

c. When was foreign involvement most influential?

You can chart your answers on a diagram like this. Decide where each period goes, noting evidence for your choice.

- Decisive involvement
- Influential involvement
- Played a part
- Insignificant impact

3   Using your answers to questions a–c, write a fuller answer to the enquiry question.

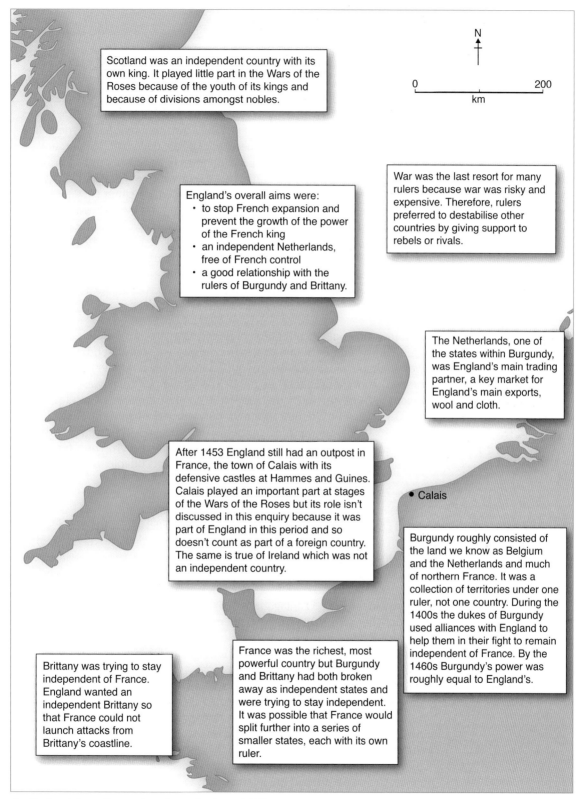

Scotland was an independent country with its own king. It played little part in the Wars of the Roses because of the youth of its kings and because of divisions amongst nobles.

N

0   200
km

War was the last resort for many rulers because war was risky and expensive. Therefore, rulers preferred to destabilise other countries by giving support to rebels or rivals.

England's overall aims were:
- to stop French expansion and prevent the growth of the power of the French king
- an independent Netherlands, free of French control
- a good relationship with the rulers of Burgundy and Brittany.

The Netherlands, one of the states within Burgundy, was England's main trading partner, a key market for England's main exports, wool and cloth.

After 1453 England still had an outpost in France, the town of Calais with its defensive castles at Hammes and Guines. Calais played an important part at stages of the Wars of the Roses but its role isn't discussed in this enquiry because it was part of England in this period and so doesn't count as part of a foreign country. The same is true of Ireland which was not an independent country.

• Calais

Burgundy roughly consisted of the land we know as Belgium and the Netherlands and much of northern France. It was a collection of territories under one ruler, not one country. During the 1400s the dukes of Burgundy used alliances with England to help them in their fight to remain independent of France. By the 1460s Burgundy's power was roughly equal to England's.

Brittany was trying to stay independent of France. England wanted an independent Brittany so that France could not launch attacks from Brittany's coastline.

France was the richest, most powerful country but Burgundy and Brittany had both broken away as independent states and were trying to stay independent. It was possible that France would split further into a series of smaller states, each with its own ruler.

△ England, her allies and rivals, in the later 1400s

1455, 1459–61

England's loss of her French empire was a vital element in the background to the battle of St Albans in 1455, but there was no direct foreign involvement in the battle or its immediate aftermath. Similarly, there was little direct involvement between 1455 and 1461, although the French raid on Sandwich in 1457 shocked rival nobles into peace-talks. During the late 1450s nobles wanted to avoid war and, when conflict began from 1459, neither side wished to be seen using foreign soldiers against their own countrymen. Charles VII of France did provide Margaret (his niece) with a little diplomatic support and Burgundy may have paid for a small contingent of Yorkist troops at Towton, but that was all. Slightly more influential was the presence of the **Papal legate**, Francesco Coppini, with the Yorkists as they landed in Kent in 1460 and marched to London. Coppini had been sent to England by the Pope to get support for a Crusade and decided, seemingly on his own initiative, that York was more likely to provide this help than Henry VI. As a result, the papal banner flew over the Yorkists as they marched through Kent. Some locals may have confused Coppini with the Archbishop of Canterbury and thought that York had the backing of the Church and therefore was in the right.

> **Papal legate**
> An ambassador sent by the Pope

1461–64

After Towton, Louis XI of France provided Margaret with diplomatic and a little military aid but did no more. His priority was not defending Margaret (even though she was a member of the French royal family) but ensuring France was not attacked by England. The danger for Louis was provoking Edward IV by giving too much aid to the Lancastrians. Scots' aid for Lancaster was of more practical help but was in Scotland's interests and not the result of 'taking sides' on behalf of Lancaster. The Scots' motive was winning the border castles of Berwick and Roxburgh. Thus, foreign aid helped to keep the Lancastrian cause alive but was unable to do more.

> And see pages 79, 83–85

1469–71

In 1470 France gave support to Warwick and Lancaster, and in 1471 Burgundy helped Edward IV but this 'choice of sides' wasn't inevitable. The choices were made in the hard-headed interests of France and Burgundy, not because of family ties or other loyalties. Louis XI backed Warwick because he wanted to destabilise Edward, who looked as if he might invade France. Importantly, Edward also looked to be in a weak position and ripe for defeat. It's doubtful if Louis would have risked antagonising Edward if he had been in a much stronger position. Therefore, Louis arranged the meeting in 1470 between Warwick and Margaret of Anjou that led to their alliance and he provided money and ships to take Warwick and his supporters back to England. Louis got what he wanted: Henry VI back on the English throne, a king who was no threat to France.

Edward fled to Burgundy but Duke Charles wasn't his natural ally, even though they were brothers-in-law. Charles also had family links to Lancaster, was a close friend of the Duke of Somerset and even had a remote claim to the English Crown of his own. And there was worse news for Edward. Charles refused to meet Edward and reportedly wished him dead! Why was Charles so anti-Edward? Charles's priority was defending Burgundy against France and so he wanted an alliance with England to bolster his own strength. It was an English alliance that was important, not who was ruling England. Therefore, he tried to negotiate with Warwick as the man ruling

> And see pages 90–92, 100–101

> Charles had married Margaret, Edward IV's sister, in 1468

England but feared that Edward's arrival in Burgundy might push Warwick into an alliance with France. In fact Edward's presence was irrelevant because Louis XI of France declared war on Burgundy in December 1470, confident of Warwick's support. Warwick was hoping to gain the rich territories of Holland and Zealand if the French attack succeeded.

Therefore, other people's decisions pushed Charles into helping Edward, not the family connection or the alliance of 1468. Charles now knew the only way he'd get English help to defend his lands was if Edward were back on the throne, so he gave Edward £20,000, ships and the facilities to prepare an invasion fleet. Edward had what he needed, thanks to Louis of France's attack on Burgundy, and this Burgundian help created the springboard for his invasion and re-conquest of his kingdom. It's worth noting that Charles still did his best to avoid antagonising France by forbidding anyone else in his territories to help Edward.

I wish Edward had never arrived. I need Warwick's help against France and Edward's presence here may frighten off Warwick.

France has declared war with Warwick's support. I need a friend on the English throne to change English policy. I'll equip Edward and help him regain his throne.

1470   **Charles of Burgundy**   **January 1471**

Perhaps surprisingly Scotland played no part in the events of 1469–71. James III was too busy establishing himself on the throne and the Scots had control of Berwick, so there was no need to take advantage of English divisions.

1483–85

During the 1470s Henry of Richmond (Henry Tudor) took refuge in Brittany, giving Duke Francis of Brittany a bargaining tool to try to get English aid for his fight to remain independent of France. During Richard III's reign, both Brittany and France and groups within these countries continued to take advantage of events in England to win support for their own aims. When Richard became king, the Duke of Brittany first sought his help against France then, realising no aid was on the way, supported Henry of Richmond's attempted invasion in October 1483 by providing him with ships. Afterwards, Brittany continued to provide a refuge for Henry and his supporters until they fled to France to avoid being handed over to Richard.

And see page 124 for details of French aid to Henry of Richmond

In France, political divisions after the death of Louis XI in August 1483 eventually played into Henry's hands. The Regent of France was facing a combined threat from Burgundy, Brittany and England, all supporting rebel nobles. To break up the opposition alliance, the Regent supported Henry's invasion in 1485 as a way of destabilising Richard. This was a success but, ironically, by the time of Bosworth, events in France were going the Regent's way. If Henry had delayed his invasion by a month, there would have been no need for France to support him in toppling Richard.

After 1485

France did take control of Brittany shortly after 1485 but the focus of European politics was turning south, away from north-western Europe, to a struggle for territory and influence in Italy. France was becoming a more stable political state, less in danger of splitting into smaller states. The European map was continuing to take shape in the late 1400s.

10 What impact did the Wars of the Roses really have?

When did the Wars of the Roses end?

Time off for good behaviour

There is no enquiry activity in this chapter. Clearly it is investigating the impact of the Wars but it's just here to be read and reflected upon. Of course, you could always develop an enquiry of your own!

Bosworth didn't end the wars. They didn't end at one specific moment but faded away slowly. Henry VII's greatest problem was the lack of confidence and security felt by nobles and gentry. In 1483 there'd been the shock of a new king 'out of the blue' and then again in 1485 with Henry himself. Why not a third new king? This thought gave any challenger hope and made men cautious about backing the King.

In 1487 Henry faced a repeat of his own invasion, headed by John de la Pole, Earl of Lincoln, nephew of Edward IV, Richard III and their sister, Margaret of Burgundy. Margaret supplied experienced mercenaries, reinforced by Irish soldiers. Briefly this invasion looked a real threat but there was little English support for the invaders and the nobility backed Henry, his army double the size of the invading force at the battle of Stoke.

Henry ploughed on, surviving what are often called Yorkist plots but were really the work of outsiders and malcontents. They had minimal support but the possibility of foreign involvement always created a sense of renewed danger. The length of time it took the wars to fade is evidence of how much uncertainty had been created by events since the 1450s.

▷ Henry VII (1485–1509). This wonderful sculpture by Pietro Torrigiano is at the Victoria and Albert Museum in London. What's remarkable is that from a distance Henry looks majestic, but move closer and you can see exhaustion and illness; the sculpture was made from his death mask.

What impact did the wars have?

This question seems simple, but you're well aware by now that questions about the wars are trickier than they seem because of the limitations of the evidence. To answer this question with certainty, we'd need evidence of how people were reacting to events but such direct evidence doesn't exist. The best we can do is to infer how people may have seen and experienced the wars. So be ready for another burst of 'probably' and 'perhaps'!

The impact of the battles

The obvious place to start is by asking 'how much fighting was there?' but historians' answers differ, depending on how they define 'fighting' (not because they can't add up). Professor Lander estimated just 12 or 13 weeks of military campaigns. Professor Goodman said 61 weeks, including armies marching to and from battles. Professor Pollard suggested over two years, including localised events such as sieges in the north east in 1462–63. However, no one argues that fighting dominated the whole period and there were many years without battles: 1456–58, 1465–68, 1472–84. This has led to the view that the wars had little impact on people because the 'quantity' of fighting was so limited.

However, doing sums does not tell the full story. It can't tell us about the psychological impact of the wars. We do have to be tentative but, though campaigns were short, it's likely their psychological impact on people was considerable. The six battles between 1459 and 1461 were spread out, but the anxiety can never have disappeared because another battle was always likely. And just when people may really have thought peace had returned, between 1471 and 1483, hope was destroyed by the upheavals of 1483 and 1485.

Estimating the numbers involved in fighting also tells us little. Most battles sound small, only 5000 at St Albans in 1455, and around 10,000 at the battles of 1471 and 1485. The numbers of casualties were therefore much smaller, but every individual killed or wounded was part of a circle of relatives and friends, which immediately widens the numbers 'involved', exactly as news of a death today devastates the immediate family and then ripples through communities. We get few glimpses of this human reality but here are two insights. In 1471 Sir John Paston and his brother, also John, fought in the Earl of Oxford's retinue at the battle of Barnet. Four days later Sir John wrote to reassure their mother:

> ... my brother John is alive and fares well and in no peril of death. He is hurt with an arrow on his right arm below his elbow. I have sent him a surgeon who has dressed the wound and he trusts he shall be well in a short time ...

This seems like a son writing an almost matter of fact letter to reduce his mother's worries, but what lay behind these calm words? What was the impact of the march to the battle, the wait for it to begin, the wound itself, wondering if it was infected, and the anxiety of the family at home, all replicated thousands of times for each conflict? Such experiences could not be quickly forgotten just because the survivors returned home.

For **Anne Herbert**
see pages 5, 53 and 139, especially the Raglan ring on page 5

And many soldiers did not return home. Anne Herbert's husband, William, was executed on Warwick's orders after the battle of Edgecote in 1469. In his will Herbert asked Anne to take the vow of chastity she'd promised to take if he died. Everything we know of her later life suggests she did.

Did the wars cause much damage?

Professor Pollard's statement that 'for <u>most of the time</u> the wars caused little suffering to <u>most of the people</u>' seems true, but the devil is in the words underlined. Not everyone was unscathed. For example, what if you'd been in Ludlow in 1459 after the Yorkist leaders fled? According to *Gregory's Chronicle*, the royal army 'when they had drunk all the wine in the taverns smote off the heads of the pipes and hogsheads of wine so men went wet-shod in wine and then they robbed the town and took away bedding, cloth and other stuff and defouled many women.'

Or if you'd been in the path of Queen Margaret's army heading south early in 1461? According to *The English Chronicle* they robbed 'all the country and people as they came, spoiling abbeys and churches and bearing away chalices, books and other ornaments'. Other sources wrote of looting of money and clothing and of farm animals driven off for food.

So, while there was little destruction overall, there was localised damage which brought considerable suffering. The general lack of damage was not accidental. Armies were on campaign only briefly and, in a civil war, looting was a major mistake, creating support and propaganda for the opposition. However, again, there's a difference between real impact and fear. An army may not have harmed anyone in its vicinity but this didn't mean local people weren't fearful. In 1460, for example, fear of fighting led the town of Hull to improve its defences. Ditches were dug, guns mounted, watch kept and an iron chain placed across the river, all leading to the town's being £210 in debt, which local people had to pay.

Impact on the nobility and gentry

We know (page 71) that there was a very high rate of involvement among nobles in the battles of 1459–61. However, when in 1471 Warwick wrote to one of his gentry retainers, Henry Vernon, 'Henry I pray you fail not now as ever I may do for you', Vernon did fail Warwick. He stayed at home rather than fight against Edward IV. Does this example suggest that nobles and gentry were more inclined to avoid involvement in warfare as time went on?

It's harder to be definite about their involvement in 1471 and 1485 because the evidence is patchy. For example, there's no evidence to show that the Yorkist Walter Devereux fought for Edward in 1471, but he probably did as Edward made him a Knight of the Garter in 1472. It is likely that men thought long and hard about fighting in 1471 and 1485 because the outcomes were unclear and because the leaders did not have such long-term claims on their loyalty as had Henry VI. It's probable that fewer nobles and gentry did fight. This does not mean they were indifferent to the country's needs but that sanity suggested caution.

It used to be said that the wars destroyed many noble families but that is not true. The greatest sufferers were those closely related to the king. Henry VI had a wide range of cousins and later there was a healthy brood of Yorkist sons, but by 1485 these royal families had been almost completely destroyed. The battles of 1459–71 and the Yorkists' tendency to murder each other had cut down the royal family to the barest Beaufort bones. Apart from the royal families, only a very few families were wiped out by battle and execution. Some others (e.g. the Hungerfords) did lose power and wealth, but perhaps the widest impact was a greater awareness that land and power could be lost if a wrong choice were made of who to support. Again, this suggests increased uncertainty and caution.

Impact on the monarchy

At the beginning of the wars respect for the monarchy was extremely high, despite Henry VI's incompetence. Despite the fighting of 1459–64 and 1469–71, there seems to have been little reduction in that respect, evidenced by Edward IV's authority in his second reign. However, the double usurpations of 1483 and 1485 may have affected the status of the monarchy. There is little sign under Richard III and Henry VII of the widespread personal loyalty felt to Henry VI and this lack of core loyalty made both kings appear insecure. What worked in their favour was not deep loyalty but more ordinary factors. Many individuals carried on their service in government because they believed this was the best way to serve the country, regardless of whether they felt great loyalty to the king. Secondly, there was general dislike of rebellion and warfare and an unwillingness to risk a family's welfare in a political cause. The status of the monarchy took time to recover from the events of 1483–85. One change increasing the monarchy's strength was that many gentry, under Edward IV and Henry VII, developed stronger direct links with the monarch as members of the royal household and so increased royal authority in the counties. By 1485 the monarch himself also had more land because a smaller royal family meant that less was given to royal relatives.

Is the internet a valuable source for studying the Wars of the Roses?

It can be, but you have to take the same care as when assessing the reliability of a historical source. Do you know who wrote the online material? Is the author an expert and objective or does s/he have an enthusiasm that leads to one-sided accounts of events or people? Is the website up to date with the latest research or based on old material? One excellent site is the *Oxford Dictionary of National Biography*. Its articles are written by named historians. You just need a local authority library membership number for access.

http://www.oxforddnb.com/public/index.html

Did people care about the wars?

▷ This graph shows changes in the value of the 'real wages' of a craftsman in relation to the population of England. This shows that the period of the wars was one of general prosperity, compared with other periods over 500 years

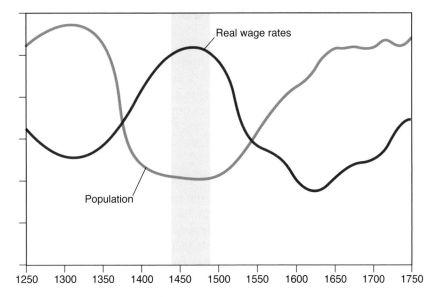

Real wage rates

Population

1250 1300 1350 1400 1450 1500 1550 1600 1650 1700 1750

Again this is a difficult question to answer, especially for the commons. We know from the documents written by Cade's rebels in 1450 that they showed considerable awareness of national politics. It seems unlikely that this awareness would have been any less over the next forty years. Supporting evidence comes from the public documents created at each crisis by leaders (York, Edward IV, Warwick, Richard of Gloucester) to win support from the merchant class and the commons. The Paston letters include numerous newsletters reporting on the latest political events, showing great interest amongst the gentry.

So, many people did care about these events but that doesn't mean the wars dominated most people's lives. Ordinary life went on as it always does and for many people this was a good time to live, one of prosperity, especially in the south and Midlands. As the graph shows, the value of wages was not only high but higher than it was to be again for many decades. Workers spent their money on better clothing, on food and on educating their children, which helped increase the level of literacy. Many larger houses and churches were expensively rebuilt, the churches with money donated by local people, especially by merchants in wool and cloth. Very importantly, William Caxton brought printing to England c.1475, one of the most significant technological developments in English history. All this suggests that England was not a country dominated by war, gloom and disaster but a country in which many people lived well. No wonder they did not want war.

Castles were built for comfort, not warfare. See pages 52–53

◁ A page from Thomas Malory's *Morte d'Arthur,* one of the first books to be printed in England. Early books looked as much like handwritten books as possible, because handwritten versions were still seen as 'the real thing' and were far more expensive. Malory wrote his stories in the 1450s and 1460s and his preoccupation with the idea of the Round Table of knights united behind King Arthur may suggest the desire to return to the 'good old days' before civil warfare broke out.

Why had battles been fought when nobody wanted civil war?

It's time to reach some conclusions to our overall question discussed on pages 11 and 72: **If loyalty was so important and people did not want civil war, why did the Wars of the Roses – with all the battles and changes of king – take place at all?**

The Victorian historians were wrong! The wars didn't happen because the monarchy, as a system, was weak or because nobles, as a group, had too much power. Instead, there's a complex mix of reasons:

- In the beginning there was a particularly weak king, Henry VI. Henry's failure to provide stability and unity allowed grievances to grow.

- Individual nobles acted out of fear to protect their positions. Fear drove actions and reactions from the 1450s.

- Feelings of insecurity increased over time. The upheavals of 1469–71 prevented the fears of the 1450s from fading. In 1471 Edward IV's return almost restored national stability but Richard III was always insecure on the throne, making further conflict likely.

- Conflicts were linked to decisions and events in other countries, where rulers wanted either to destabilise or to support English kings for their own reasons.

- Two individuals, Warwick and Richard of Gloucester, had unexpected reactions to difficult situations. We can't be certain of their motives but each man took a first step, unable to foresee the consequences of that action, and found himself carried onwards by events and other people's reactions.

- Loyalty itself led to conflict. The conflict of 1483–85 arose not solely out of Richard III's actions but also from the resistance of members of Edward IV's household, loyal to young Edward V.

It's the complexity of the factors and the way they became entangled that overwhelmed the general desire for peace, a situation that has recurred time and time again in history.

In examining individuals' motives for their actions we have to remember one thing: these were real, individual people who shared principles and ideals. We can only begin to understand their choices and actions if we respect the people we study. In her book *The Wars of the Roses*, Professor Carpenter rightly identifies the importance of:

> ... respecting the people we study; not deriding them for having beliefs we do not share nor dismissing them as aliens who share nothing with us at all. If the apparently incoherent politics of the last sixty years of the fifteenth century are studied as a period in which human beings with certain kinds of expectations were suddenly confronted with the wholly unexpected and struggled to understand and to cope with it, as human beings will, they begin to make a surprising amount of sense.

Respect, not derision, is what we owe the past. Our understanding of the Wars of the Roses has moved on a long way. It will keep improving if we respect the people of the time, which brings us to our last two pages.

Were people then so very different from us?

△ A reconstruction drawing by Ivan Lapper of Fountain's Court at Raglan Castle in the 1460s. William and Anne Herbert rebuilt Raglan (see page 53) to reflect William's power. He dominated Wales for Edward IV, their son married one of Queen Elizabeth's sisters, and William was the first Welshman to be made an earl.

The people in the picture don't look very like us. Their clothes are certainly different! And when we quickly compare then and now many other differences are obvious. They had no electricity, no anaesthetics, no cars. Their lives revolved around the farming year. They wrote about 'the Saturday next before St Margaret's Day', not Saturday 18 July. They can't have been like us at all. And there's one more thing: can you imagine fighting in armour, swinging a poll-axe to kill another man? For a long time that seemed to me the biggest difference, the acceptance of learning to kill another human being at close range.

And then one day I was looking at a photograph of my Dad, in the army, in Burma in 1943. Until he was 26, he'd spent his spare time playing sports, a cricket bat the nearest he'd come to a weapon. Then in 1939 he joined the Army and was taught to use a bayonet and to kill people. I don't know if he did. He never talked about his war-years, though just once he briefly described wading through swamps, bayonet fixed, waiting for an attack.

And my grandfather went through the same experience, from clerk to soldier, in the Great War. So, perhaps the differences, the real human differences, aren't as great as I thought. We can never really know, but perhaps we have more in common with the people of the fifteenth century than we might think. Listen to this mother – she sounds like she could be mine or yours – but it's actually Agnes Paston nagging her son John in 1443:

be well dieted of meat and drink, for that is the greatest help that you may have now to your health ward.

In other words, eat properly and look after yourself!

What about friendship? This may seem a strange topic to end with when we've been studying wars famed for battles and never-ending feuds. But was everyone consumed by hatred? Some people were, but fewer perhaps than we might think. This final instalment of Anne Herbert's story (see pages 5, 53 and 134) tells a different tale. It's the story of the two women below, who once stood talking in the courtyard of Raglan Castle, just like the people in the picture opposite.

△ Anne Herbert, Countess of Pembroke. Her brother, Walter Devereux, died at Bosworth fighting against Henry VII.

△ Margaret Beaufort, mother of Henry VII. She is often portrayed as a real Lancastrian harridan, ruthlessly plotting and conniving for her son to become king.

It's easy to assume that these two women hated each other. Anne's brother was killed fighting against Margaret's son. Yet the evidence suggests they were friends. Back in the 1460s Anne and her husband had brought up Margaret's son, young Henry of Richmond (Henry VII) alongside their sons, William and Walter. Documents record Margaret visiting Raglan and the Herberts planned that young Henry would marry their daughter, Maud. However, when Edward IV returned in 1471, Henry was taken to Brittany. Maud married the Earl of Northumberland instead.

Anne did not meet Henry again until days after Bosworth when she was summoned to meet the new king. I'd bet a decent sum that it was a friendly meeting and that Henry's mother, Margaret Beaufort, was there. Why? It seems that Anne and Margaret had built a lasting friendship. There are no letters to prove this, just one intriguing clue. Twenty years later, Margaret owned a palace at Collyweston. Though Anne had died by then, Margaret kept rooms in her palace for one of Anne's daughters. That suggests a bond between the families, a sign of Margaret's gratitude to the Herberts for their care in bringing up her son.

This seems a good place to end, with two women who became friends despite the violence around them; a reminder of the qualities shared by people across time and place, a reminder of the humanity we share with the people who lived through the Wars of the Roses.

Index

Entries in **bold** refer to glossary terms